PRINCIPLES AND PERSONALITIES

An Easy-to-Read Reference Guide to the People and Ideas That Formed Alcoholics Anonymous

Orrin R. Onken

Salish Ponds Press LLC

ISBN-13: 978-0-9824564-6-0

ISBN-10: 0-9824564-6-8

Disclaimer

This book, *Principles and Personalities*, is an independent work of history and biography. It is not approved, endorsed, or authorized by Alcoholics Anonymous World Services, Inc. (AAWS) or the General Service Office (GSO).

The terms "Alcoholics Anonymous," "AA," and "The Big Book" are registered trademarks of Alcoholics Anonymous World Services, Inc. These terms are used in this book solely for historical reference and descriptive purposes under the principles of "Fair Use." The views expressed here are those of the author and do not represent the official position of the fellowship of Alcoholics Anonymous.

Printed in the United States of America First Edition

How to Use This Handbook

Welcome! Whether you are brand new to Alcoholics Anonymous or have been around for a long time, this book was written for you. History books are often dry or difficult to read, but this handbook is different. It is broken into small, easy-to-digest chapters that tell the story of the people and events that made AA possible.

There is no wrong way to use this book. Think of it as both a **story** and a **toolbox**.

1. The Story Method (Reading Front-to-Back)

If you want to see how the miracle happened, start at page one and simply enjoy the story of AA as it emerges from the biographies of the founders and the descriptions of events.

2. The Reference Method (Pick and Choose)

If you hear a name in a meeting—like "Sister Ignatia," "Ebby T.," or "Marty Mann"—and want to know who they are, you can flip directly to their biography.

- **Self-Contained Chapters:** Each story is written to stand on its own, so you don't

- have to read the whole book to understand one person.
- **The Glossary:** If you hear a term like "DCM" or "The Seventh Tradition," use the glossary at the back for a simple explanation.

Table of Contents

A Two-Minute History of Alcoholics Anonymous

Alcoholics Anonymous (AA) began with a simple idea: that one alcoholic talking to another could achieve what doctors, priests, and family members could not. The story began when two "hopeless" men in Ohio met across a kitchen table. From there it grew into a worldwide movement that has saved millions of lives.

Bill Wilson's Struggle with Alcoholism

Bill Wilson, the primary author of the Big Book, *Alcoholics Anonymous*, was a man who found great success on Wall Street as a stock trader and investigator. He was good at studying businesses, but by the early 1930s, his life was falling apart because of his drinking. Bill had been hospitalized many times. His doctors told his wife, Lois, that he would either die or go insane if he didn't stop drinking.

In 1934, Bill had a visit from an old friend named Ebby. Bill expected Ebby to be a drinking companion, but Ebby was sober. He told Bill that he had found a way to stay dry through the Oxford Group, a religious movement of the time that practiced honesty, unselfishness, and helping others. Bill was doubtful that religion could help him. Ebby told Bill, "Why don't you choose your own concept of God?" This simple idea—

that a person didn't have to follow a specific religion to be spiritual—stayed with Bill.

Soon after, Bill went back to the hospital for the last time. There, he had a powerful spiritual experience. He felt a brilliant light and a sense of peace. He never took another drink for the rest of his life.

Bill Meets Dr. Bob in Akron

In May 1935, while on a business trip in Akron, Ohio, Bill felt the urge to drink after a failed business deal. Instead of going to the bar, he went to a church directory and started making phone calls. He wasn't looking for a drink; he was looking for another alcoholic to talk to.

He reached Henrietta Seiberling, a member of the Akron Oxford Group. She introduced Bill to Dr. Bob Smith, a local surgeon who was also struggling with a drinking problem. Dr. Bob was skeptical. He told his wife he would give this "New York talker" only fifteen minutes. That fifteen-minute meeting lasted for hours. On June 10, 1935, Dr. Bob had his last drink. That day is celebrated as the official birthday of Alcoholics Anonymous.

The Fellowship of AA Expands

For the next few years, Bill and Bob worked tirelessly. They realized that their method worked best when they focused on the medical reality of alcoholism—that it was an illness of the body and the mind that required a spiritual solution.

At first, Bill and Bob worked with the Oxford Group. Later they decided that the Oxford Group rules were too strict. Alcoholics needed a place where they could be honest about their failures. In 1937, the groups in New York and Akron struck out on their own. There were about 40 members who were staying sober.

Writing the "Big Book"

By 1938, the early members realized that if they wanted to help people outside of New York and Akron, they needed to put their experience into writing. Bill W. began writing the book *Alcoholics Anonymous.*

The early members argued over every word. Some wanted the book to be very religious, while others wanted it to be purely scientific. Bill chose a balanced approach. He wanted the book to be inclusive so that anyone, regardless of their beliefs, could find help.

One of the most important parts of the book was the Twelve Steps. Bill wrote them quickly one night, expanding on the ideas the members had been using in their meetings. These steps provided a clear path for recovery: admitting powerlessness, seeking help from a power greater than ourselves, cleaning up the past, and helping others.

The book was published in 1939. Because of its thick paper and large size, it was nicknamed the "Big Book." It was published by Works Publishing, a company the member started themselves because no major publisher would take a chance on a book for drunks.

Early Struggles and Growing Pains

At first, the book didn't sell well. The fellowship was broke and struggling. Two events changed everything. First, an article in Liberty magazine brought in hundreds of inquiries. Second, and most importantly, in 1941, the Saturday Evening Post published a long article by Jack Alexander.

Suddenly, thousands of people across the country were writing letters asking for help. AA exploded from a few hundred members to several thousand in just a few months.

As AA grew, it faced growing pains. People argued about money, leadership, and who should be allowed to join. Bill W. watched these fights and realized that the fellowship needed a set of principles to stay united. He developed the Twelve Traditions. These rules ensured that AA would never have professional leaders, never take outside money, and always remain anonymous at the level of press, radio, and film.

AA Spreads Across the Globe

In 1950, Dr. Bob died, but the foundation he and Bill had built was solid. In 1955 a convention was held. Bill asked the members to take responsibility for the future of the program, and the delegates voted to accept this duty. This vote made the General Service Conference the permanent link between the groups and the trustees. AA no longer belonged to the founders; it belonged to every alcoholic who reached out for help.

Today, Alcoholics Anonymous is active in almost every country in the world. The Big Book has been translated into over 70 languages. The core message remains the same as it was in that Akron living room in 1935: when one alcoholic shares their story with another, the miracle of recovery begins.

The Legacy of AA

The history of AA is not just the history of an organization; it is a history of a change in how the world sees alcoholism. It moved the conversation from shame and punishment to empathy and healing. It proved that even when a person feels hopeless, there is always a way back.

Part 1: The People Who Were There When It All Started

Bill Wilson

The Man Who Wrote the Twelve Steps

Bill Wilson was the primary author of the Big Book, *Alcoholics Anonymous*. To millions of people, he is known simply as "Bill W." Working with other alcoholics, he found a solution for the suffering alcoholic and spent the rest of his life sharing that solution with anyone who needed it.

The Early Years: A Drive to Succeed

Bill was born in 1895 in a small town in Vermont. His childhood was not easy. His parents divorced when he was young, which was very unusual in those days. He was raised mostly by his grandparents. Even as a young boy, Bill had a strong drive to succeed.

Bill decided he would be the best at everything he tried. He spent months learning how to make a boomerang because he heard it was hard to do. He learned to play the violin and became a leader in his school. On the outside, he looked successful and confident. On the inside, he often felt lonely and afraid that he wasn't good enough.

World War I and Bill's First Experience of Drinking

When World War I broke out, Bill joined the army and became an officer. While he was training in Massachusetts, he was invited to a party. It was there that he had his first drink of alcohol—a cocktail called a Bronx.

At first, it seemed like a miracle. Bill was often shy and felt like he didn't fit in with other people. Alcohol made those feelings go away. It made him feel like he was part of the group. It made him powerful and relaxed. He had finally found the secret to life that everyone else already knew. For Bill, drinking wasn't just a hobby; it was medicine for his soul.

Success and then a Downward Spiral

After the war, Bill moved to New York City with his wife, Lois. He was smart and had a talent for understanding the stock market. He would travel around the country looking at factories and then advise people in New York which stocks to buy. For a while, he was earning a lot of money.

But his drinking was starting to become a problem. What started as a way to feel confident became something he could not control. He would show up to important meetings drunk. He became unreliable. Even when the stock market crashed in 1929 and he lost his money, he couldn't stop drinking. He tried to blame his problems on the economy or bad luck, but the truth was that alcohol had taken over his life.

By the early 1930s, Bill was a "broken man." He and Lois had to move into her parents' house. He spent his days walking the streets, looking for money to buy a bottle. He made solemn promises to Lois, he went to hospitals for the cure, and he tried to use his own willpower. Nothing worked. He would stay sober a little while, but the terrible urge would always come back. He felt as if he were under a spell he couldn't break.

The Message from Ebby Thacher

In 1934, an old friend named Ebby Thacher came to visit Bill. Ebby had been a heavy drinker too—someone Bill had often gotten drunk with. But Ebby was sober and looked healthy. Bill was surprised and offered him a drink. Ebby refused. He told Bill that he had found religion in a group called the Oxford Group.

Ebby explained that to stop drinking, Bill didn't have to follow a specific religion. He simply had to admit he was beaten, get honest with himself, and ask a Higher Power for help. Bill was skeptical. He didn't like the idea of religion or God. But Ebby said something that changed everything: "Why don't you choose your own conception of God?" This meant Bill could choose a power that made sense to him.

A Turning Point at Towns Hospital

A few days later, Bill went back to Towns Hospital in New York. He was at the end of his rope. While lying in bed, he felt a deep sense of despair. He cried out, "If there be a God, let Him show Himself now!"

Suddenly, the room lit up with a bright light. Bill felt a sense of peace he had never known. He felt as though he was standing on a mountaintop and a wind was blowing through him. It wasn't a wind composed of air, but a wind of spirit. He felt like he was finally free.

The doctor at the hospital, Dr. Silkworth, told Bill not to be afraid of the experience. He told Bill that whatever had happened, he should hold onto it, because it was better than the life he had been living. Bill never took another drink of alcohol for the rest of his life.

Akron and the Meeting with Dr. Bob

Bill realized that staying sober required two things: a connection to a Higher Power and helping other alcoholics. In 1935, Bill was on a business trip in Akron, Ohio. The business deal failed, and Bill felt lonely and frustrated. He stood in the lobby of the Mayflower Hotel and looked at the bar. He had the urge to drink.

He knew that to stay sober, he needed to talk to another alcoholic. He made several phone calls and was finally introduced to Dr. Bob Smith, a local surgeon who was also struggling with drink. Dr. Bob only agreed to give Bill 15 minutes of his time. But when they started talking, they found they had so much in common that they talked for hours.

They realized that when one alcoholic talks to another, they can reach each other in a way that doctors and priests cannot. Dr. Bob took his last drink on June 10, 1935.

Writing the Big Book: A Team Effort

In 1938, Bill began writing the book *Alcoholics Anonymous*. He wanted to put down on paper exactly how they had recovered. Bill was the main writer, but he had a lot of help from a small team in New York. Bill was the creative source of the Twelve Steps.

One of the most important people in AA at this time was Henry "Hank" Parkhurst. Hank was a businessman who had also found sobriety. He was very bold and had a can-do attitude. He helped Bill organize the business side of publishing the book. Hank also wrote the chapter in the book called "To Employers," which gave advice to bosses on how to help alcoholic workers.

Another key person was Ruth Hock. Ruth was not an alcoholic, but she was a loyal friend to the early AA members. She worked as Bill and Hank's secretary. At that time, there were no computers, so Ruth produced every word of the manuscript on a typewriter. She often typed and re-typed chapters as Bill and the others made changes. Ruth kept the files organized and made sure that Bill's messy handwriting became a readable book.

Bill sent chapters to the members in New York and Akron. They argued over every phrase. Some members wanted the book to be very religious, while others wanted it to be highly scientific. Because of these debates, Bill settled on language that was inclusive, adopting the phrase "God *as we understood Him.*" This made it possible for anyone to use the program. The book was published in 1939 and became the textbook for recovery.

The Twelve Traditions

As AA grew, it faced many problems. Groups argued about money, leadership, and fame. Bill realized that just as the individual needs the Twelve Steps to stay sober, the group needs rules to stay together. He wrote the Twelve Traditions. These rules said that AA should never take outside money, should not be part of politics, and that members should remain anonymous in the media.

Bill became a very famous man, but he lived by these traditions. He refused to have his picture taken for magazines like *Time*. He refused to take money for his leadership in AA. He wanted the program to belong to the members, not to him.

In his later years, Bill struggled with depression and health issues. Even when he felt bad, he remained honest about his feelings. He showed that being sober didn't mean life would be perfect. It meant having the tools to handle life without turning to a bottle.

Bill Wilson died on January 24, 1971. By his death, AA had spread to almost every country in the world. Millions of people were living happy, useful lives because Bill was willing to share his story and the solution.

Dr. Bob Smith

The Co-Founder of Alcoholics Anonymous

In the history of Alcoholics Anonymous, Bill W. was the salesman and writer. Bill spread the program across the country and the globe. Dr. Bob was a doctor who stayed in one place and made his contribution helping people, one on one.

Bob's Early Years

Robert Holbrook Smith was born in 1879 in St. Johnsbury, Vermont. He grew up in a very religious home. His parents were good people, but they were very strict. Bob had to go to church services many times a week. This made him dislike religion. He was smart and a hard worker. He went to college at Dartmouth, and that is where his trouble with drinking began.

In college, Bob could drink more than most people. He liked the way it made him feel. It helped him feel less shy and more like one of the boys. Early on, he noticed that drinking affected him differently than it did others. He had frequent blackouts, but because he was young and strong, he kept on drinking.

Bob's Struggle to Become a Doctor

Bob wanted to be a doctor. He enrolled in medical school, but his drinking held him back. He missed classes and failed tests because of hangovers. At one point, he dropped out of school for a while. Eventually, he finished his studies and became a surgeon in Akron, Ohio. He married a kind woman named Anne Ripley, and they had two children.

On the outside, Dr. Bob was a successful and talented surgeon. But on the inside, he was dying. He tried everything to stop drinking. He went to hospitals. He stayed in drying out places. He made promises to Anne. He read the Bible, but nothing worked. For seventeen years, he would stay sober just enough to perform surgery, but as soon as the work was done, he would head home to drink to oblivion. He became terrified that he would lose his medical license or kill a patient.

The Oxford Group and a Meeting With Bill W.

In the early 1930s, Dr. Bob and Anne joined a group called the Oxford Group. These were people who tried to live by very high spiritual standards. Dr. Bob went to their meetings for two years, but he still couldn't stay sober. He knew the rules of how to live, but he didn't have the power to follow them.

Then came Mother's Day in 1935. A man named Bill W. was in Akron on a business trip. Bill was a recovered alcoholic from New York. He was having a hard time and felt like he needed to talk to another alcoholic to keep himself from drinking. Through a series of phone calls, he was put in touch with Dr. Bob's friends.

At first, Dr. Bob didn't want to meet Bill. He was hungover and tired. He told Anne he would give the man fifteen minutes. That fifteen minutes turned into hours. For the first time, Dr. Bob was talking to someone who really understood what it felt like to be a hopeless drunk. Bill didn't preach to him. Bill just shared his own experience.

Bob's Last Drink

After meeting Bill, Dr. Bob continued to drink for several weeks. He went to a medical convention and got very drunk. When he came home, Bill helped him detox. On June 10, 1935, Dr. Bob had his last drink—a beer given to him by Bill to steady his hands so he could perform surgery that morning. The date of Dr. Bob's last drink is now celebrated as the anniversary of AA.

Hard Times and Helping Hands

In the early days of AA, things were tough for Dr. Bob. Because of his years of drinking, his medical practice was almost gone. He was broke and owed a lot of money. While he never charged people for AA help, he and Bill W. needed a way to live so they could keep building the fellowship.

A group called the Alcoholic Foundation was set up to help. Wealthy friends, including John D. Rockefeller Jr., gave some money to a trust. Because he was spending almost all his time helping others for free, Bob had no way to earn a living. This trust paid Dr. Bob a stipend of $30 a week. This was not a salary for his AA work, but a way to keep his family fed and his lights on while he and Bill built the program. Later, when the Big Book began to sell, he received some money from the book sales. This allowed him to spend his time doing the work that saved so many lives. Even with this financial help, he lived a simple life and never became a rich man.

Dr. Bob's Contribution to the Big Book

Dr. Bob and Bill W. started working together to help other alcoholics at the Akron City Hospital. By helping others, they stayed sober themselves. This was the piece that the Oxford Group had not been able to provide.

When it came time to write the Big Book, Dr. Bob played an essential role. He was the one who insisted that the program stay simple. Bill W. liked to use big words and complex ideas. Dr. Bob always said, "Let's not lousc this thing up with complex grammar." IIe wanted the message to be clear enough for anyone to understand.

In the Big Book, Dr. Bob wrote the story titled "Doctor Bob's Nightmare." It contains one of the most famous pieces of advice in AA history. He says that the spiritual life is not a theory, but something we have to live. He told his fellow alcoholics that if we want to stay sober, we have to trust God, clean house, and help others.

Dr. Bob's Legacy of Service

Dr. Bob spent the rest of his life serving others. He and Anne turned their home into a place where alcoholics could come to get well. It is estimated that Dr. Bob personally helped over 5,000 alcoholics before he passed away.

In his final years, when very sick with cancer, he kept on working. His last message to the fellowship at a convention in 1950 was very short and simple. He told the members to "Keep it simple." He warned against getting too proud or making the program too complicated.

Dr. Bob died on November 16, 1950. He taught us that the best way to keep the gift of sobriety is to give it away to someone else.

Henry Parkhurst

The Founder Who Didn't Stay Sober

Most people know the names of Bill Wilson and Dr. Bob Smith. But there was a third man who was just as important in the very beginning. His name was Henry Parkhurst, often called "Hank P." by the early members.

Who Was Henry Parkhurst?

Henry Parkhurst was a businessman from New Jersey. He was a natural salesman. He had a lot of energy and big ideas. Before his drinking became a problem, he ran a company called Honor Dealers. The business helped gas station owners join together to buy supplies at a discount. Ruth Hock, the woman who typed the first draft of the Big Book, was a secretary for Honor Dealers.

Henry was energetic, hard-working, and talented, but he never truly succeeded in business or in life due to his drinking.

Henry Gets Sober

In 1935, Henry met Bill Wilson. AA did not have a name yet. It was just a small group of people in New York and Akron who were trying to stay sober by helping each other.

For a few years, Henry was a powerhouse in the program. He was excited about sobriety, and used his business skills to help the small group of drunks stay organized. He was a close friend to Bill Wilson, and for a while, they were partners in a great mission.

A Partner in Writing the Big Book

By 1938, the group decided they needed to write a book to share their message with the world. Henry played a huge role in this.

Henry was still running Honor Dealers, so he provided the office space in Newark, New Jersey. In that office, he and Bill and Ruth Hock began work on the Big Book. Bill dictated over Ruth's shoulder, and Ruth typed.

Henry did more than just provide an office; he was a co-writer. While Bill Wilson wrote most of the book, Henry is the author of the chapter "To Employers." Having been a high-level executive, Henry knew how to talk to bosses about the problem employee. He wanted to show businesses that an alcoholic who found sobriety could become a loyal and hard-working worker.

Author of the Story, "The Unbeliever"

Henry's influence on the Big Book included more than just writing the chapter 'To Employers." His story, "The

Unbeliever" was the very first story in the first edition of the Big Book.

In his story, Henry shared his personal journey and his struggle with the idea of God. Because he was a man of science and logic, he found the spiritual part of the program difficult. By putting his story first, the early members hoped to show other non-religious people that they, too, could find sobriety.

Henry's Story is Removed from Later Editions

A few months after the publication of the first edition of the Big Book, Henry returned to drinking. It was a difficult time for the early members. Sales of the book were not good. Honor Dealers, Henry's business, went bankrupt, and tension developed between Bill and Henry.

When the second edition was published in 1955, Henry's story was removed.

Most historians believe this was because Henry had returned to drinking and was no longer active in the program. Members felt it was important that the personal stories in the back of the book were written by people who were still sober and living the AA way of life.

The "Big" in the Big Book

Henry was always the salesman and wanted the book

to look like a great value. He was the one who suggested using very thick paper and large margins so that people felt they were getting a lot for their money. It is still called the Big Book today because of Henry's marketing idea.

He also helped start Works Publishing, a private business used to sell the book. In 1940 all the stockholders of Works Publishing, including Hank, were bought out by a non-profit foundation that had supported AA from the beginning. After a couple of name changes that company became AA World Services, Inc.

Henry spent the rest of his life going in and out of sobriety. He never fully found the peace that the Big Book describes. He died in 1954.

Why Henry is Worth Remembering

Henry Parkhurst never achieved long-term sobriety, ut his contributions to early AA are undeniable. He provided the office space, a secretary, and much of the organization that made production of the book possible. He was responsible for the physical look of the first Big Book and contributed an important chapter, "To Employers" that still exists today.

Henry Parkhurst was a man of great talent and great flaws. We remember him with gratitude for the hard work he did to help start AA and propel it into the world.

Lois Wilson

The Wife of Bill Wilson and Founder of Al-Anon

Lois Wilson was the wife of Bill Wilson and an important person in the history of AA in her own right. She stood beside Bill during the worst of his drinking. She worked to support the couple when he could not. Later, as Bill threw himself into the work of building Alcoholics Anonymous, she turned her attention to the suffering families of alcoholics. Her life is a story of great patience, deep love, and dedication to helping others.

A Marriage With So Much Promise

Lois Burnham was born in 1891 in Brooklyn, New York. She grew up in a loving, stable home. Her father was a well-known doctor, and her family spent their summers in Vermont. It was there, in the beautiful green mountains, that she met a tall, ambitious young man named Bill Wilson.

The two fell in love and married in 1918, just before Bill went overseas to fight in World War I. Their life was full of promise. Bill was smart and destined for success in the business world. Lois was a trained nurse and an artist. They had dreams of travel, a home, and a family. But soon, Bill's drinking cast a shadow over everything.

The Dark Years

For many years, Lois watched the man she loved disappear into alcoholism. Bill's drinking wasn't just a bad habit. It was a sickness that took over their lives. He lost jobs, they lost their home, and they lost their savings.

Lois did everything she could to save him. She pleaded, she scolded, and she hid his bottles. She took on extra work to pay the bills. She stayed by his side when he was in the hospital, and she hoped every time he promised to stop that this time would be different. Like so many people who love an alcoholic, Lois felt lonely, ashamed, and afraid. She thought that if she could just be a better wife or work harder, Bill would stop. She didn't understand that she was powerless over his drinking.

The Breaking Point for Lois

Everything changed in late 1934. Bill had a powerful spiritual experience and finally stopped drinking. At first, Lois was overjoyed. Her prayers had been answered. But soon, a fresh problem came up. Bill was so busy trying to help other alcoholics stay sober he was hardly ever home. When he was home, the house was filled with drunks.

Lois felt left out. She had stayed with Bill through all the bad years, and now that he was sober, he seemed to care more about his new friends in AA than he did about her. She was resentful.

One day, while Bill was getting ready to go to a meeting, Lois snapped. She threw a shoe at him and shouted that she hated his meetings. That moment was a turning point. She realized she had been living her life through him. She needed to find her own spiritual path.

The Birth of Al-Anon

Lois talked to the wives of the other men in the early AA groups. She found out they were feeling the same things she was: anger, hurt, and loneliness. The wives realized they needed the same solution that their husbands were using. They needed to learn how to let go, how to stop trying to control others, and how to focus on their own growth.

For years, these family groups grew slowly and separately. In 1951, Lois and her friend Anne Binney decided it was time to bring them all together. They opened an office in the basement of Lois and Bill's home, a place called Stepping Stones. They named this new fellowship Al-Anon Family Groups.

Lois insisted that Al-Anon stay separate from AA. Families needed their own space to heal. She worked tirelessly, answering letters from all over the world and helping people start their own groups. She showed people that even if the alcoholic in their life was still drinking, they could still find peace and joy for themselves.

The Big Book and the Chapter "To Wives."

When the Big Book was being written, Lois assumed she would be allowed to write the chapter "To Wives." Bill did not allow her to do that, and his decision terribly hurt her. Instead, Bill wrote it from the perspective of an alcoholic telling wives how to behave. Lois thought, and many people agree, that what Bill wrote was patronizing and condescending toward wives.

Lois and the Spread of Al-Anon

Bill died in 1971, but Lois continued her work for many more years. She traveled the world, speaking to thousands of people and spreading the message of Al-Anon. She remained humble, always seeing herself as just another person trying to live by spiritual principles.

Lois passed away in 1988 at the age of 97. By then, Al-Anon had grown into a worldwide fellowship with tens of thousands of groups.

Anne Ripley Smith

The Mother of AA

AA might not have survived its first summer without the calm and unwavering presence of Anne Smith. She was the wife of Dr. Bob, but much more than that. Without her quiet strength and deep faith, the program we know today might never have survived.

A Girl from Illinois

Anne Ripley was born in 1881 in Oak Park, Illinois. She grew up in a comfortable, loving home. She was well-educated, patient, and had a deep interest in spiritual matters from a young age.

She met Robert Holbrook Smith (Dr. Bob) while he was a young medical student. They fell in love and were married in 1915. At the time, Bob was a doctor, and Anne looked forward to life as a surgeon's wife in Akron, Ohio. They soon had two children, a son named Smitty and a daughter named Sue.

The Dark Years of Dr. Bob's Alcoholism

Anne's vision of a carefree marriage was not to be. For close to two decades, Anne watched the man she loved disappear behind a fog of alcohol.

Bob was a periodic drinker at first, but graduated to drinking every day. He would perform surgery during the day, often shaking, and then drink himself into a stupor at night. Anne spent countless nights waiting for him to come home, wondering if he was safe. She hid the car keys, paid the bills he forgot to pay, and kept up appearances so the neighbors wouldn't know the truth.

Despite her fear and loneliness, Anne never gave up on Bob. She didn't stay because she was weak; she stayed because she believed that underneath the illness, Bob was still a good man. She had a deep faith that God had a plan.

A Search for Answers in the Oxford Group

In the early 1930s, she started looking for help in meetings of the Akron Oxford Group. The group was associated with the Congregational Church, and was a Christian movement that believed in practicing honesty, purity, unselfishness, and love. The members also believed in quiet time, where a person would sit still and listen for God's guidance.

Anne brought Bob to these meetings, hoping they would help him leave alcohol alone. Bob attended for two and a half years but never stopped drinking. Anne kept praying, kept studying, and kept believing.

The Meeting That Changed Everything

In May 1935, Bill Wilson came to Akron. He was lonely and tempted to drink, so he called a local minister to find another drunk to talk to. That call led him to Henrietta Seiberling, the leader of the Akron Oxford Group attended by Bob and Anne.

On Mother's Day, 1935, Bill and Bob met at Henrietta's house. They talked for hours. For the first time, Bob met someone who understood exactly how he felt. Anne and Henrietta sat in the kitchen, giving them space. Bob took his last drink on June 10, 1935, and a new way of life began for the Smith family.

The Kitchen Table Ministry

Once Bob got sober, the Smiths' home at 855 Ardmore Avenue became the center of the new movement. Because there were no hospitals or rehabs for alcoholics back then, Anne and Bob brought the men into their own home.

For the next several years, Anne Smith's house was a spiritual hospital. At any given time, there might be three or four alcoholics living in their spare rooms. Anne did the laundry, cooked the meals, and sat with the wives of these men.

The AA Kitchen Table became famous. While the men were in the living room talking about how to stay sober, Anne was in the kitchen with the wives, teaching them how to find their own spiritual peace.

Anne's Journals and the Big Book

Anne was a student of the Bible and spiritual literature. She kept detailed journals of her thoughts and the lessons she learned during her quiet time. She shared these lessons with the early members of AA every morning.

When Bill Wilson began writing the Big Book, many of the spiritual ideas he included came from Anne. She emphasized the importance of humility, the need to make amends, and the power of daily prayer. Besides editing early drafts of the Big Book, she reminded the early members that love and service were the keys to staying sober.

Anne and Bob's Home Becomes a National Monument

Anne Smith passed away in 1949, just a year before Dr. Bob. By that time, Alcoholics Anonymous had grown from a small group in her living room to a worldwide fellowship of thousands.

Anne never wanted the spotlight, but today the home she lived in with Bob is a National Historic Landmark. It is preserved to look as it did in the 1930s and 40s, where visitors can see the famous kitchen table where so many were helped. The site has expanded into a small campus, and every June, thousands of people from around the world travel to Akron for Founders'

Day to visit the place where it all began.

Part 2: Early Members of the Fellowship

Bill Dotson

The Man on the Bed

Shortly after Dr. Bob got sober in June 1935, he and Bill W. realized they needed to pass it on to stay sober themselves. They went to Akron City Hospital and found Bill Dotson, a well-known city councilman and attorney who was strapped to a bed in the alcoholic ward.

Bill Dotson became the third member of Alcoholics Anonymous. His personal story is told in the Big Book with the title, "Alcoholic Number Three," and his meeting with Bill W. and Dr. Bob is the subject of the famous AA painting, "The Man on the Bed."

A Man of Promise

Bill Dotson was born in 1892. As a young man, he had everything going for him. He was a well-known lawyer in Akron, Ohio, and a veteran of World War I. He had a devoted wife. He was a leader in his church and a respected member of his community.

From the outside, Bill was a success. But Bill had a secret that was slowly destroying his life. Bill could not control his drinking. What started as social drinking turned into a habit, and the habit had turned into an obsession.

The Downward Spiral

Bill was not a skid row drunk, at least not at first. He was a high-bottom alcoholic who tried many times to stop. He went to hospitals. He made promises to his family and prayed for help in his church.

But as soon as Bill got out of the hospital, or as soon as the memory of his last bad night faded, he would pick up a drink again. He felt a deep sense of shame that he knew how to argue a court case but couldn't argue himself out of a drink. In the summer of 1935, Bill was in Akron City Hospital again, this time in a room for patients who were violent.

The Meeting That Changed Everything

While Bill was lying in that hospital bed in Akron, two men came to see him. One was Dr. Bob Smith, a local doctor Bill knew by reputation. The other was a man from New York named Bill Wilson.

Bill W. and Dr. Bob had only been sober for a short time themselves. They hadn't come to the hospital to preach to Bill Dotson or to tell him he was a bad person. They told him their own stories. They talked about their own failures, their cravings, and the mental twist that always led them back to the bottle.

For the first time in his life, Bill Dotson didn't feel judged. He felt understood. These men weren't looking down on him; they had been exactly where he was.

They explained that alcoholism was a sickness of the mind, body, and spirit.

Bill Dotson listened, but he was skeptical. Bill W. and Dr. Bob kept talking. They told him they had found a way to stay sober by trusting in a power greater than themselves and by trying to help other alcoholics. They told him that if he wanted to stay sober, he had to tell his story to someone else.

The Breakthrough

On the third day of their visits, something clicked for Bill Dotson. He realized that if these two men could stay sober by talking to him, maybe he could stay sober by talking to the next person. He wasn't just a patient being helped; he was a link in a chain.

Bill Dotson got out of bed and walked into a new life. He never took another drink for the rest of his life.

His recovery was a turning point for the early AA group. Before Bill Dotson, it was just Bill W. and Dr. Bob. People might have said, "Well, maybe those two just got lucky." But when Bill Dotson got sober and stayed sober, it proved that the AA thing was a program that could be taught and shared.

Bill Dotson in Sobriety

Bill Dotson went back to being a lawyer, but his real work became helping other alcoholics. He was known for being kind but also firm about the program. He emphasized the spiritual side of recovery. His life had been saved by a power he couldn't explain, and he spent his days trying to honor that gift.

Bill remained active in the Akron AA community for many years. He was a living example of the fact that no matter how many times you have been to the hospital, and no matter how much you have lost, you can still recover.

His Legacy

Bill Dotson passed away in 1954. At the time of his death, he had been sober for over 19 years. By then, Alcoholics Anonymous had grown from three men in Akron to hundreds of thousands of people all over the world.

Bill's contribution to AA is often remembered during the Founders' Day celebrations. He represents all who come into the rooms feeling like they are at the end of the road.

In 1955 an illustrator named Robert M. painted the picture that came to be known as "The Man on the Bed." In it, Bill W. and Dr. Bob sit at the bedside of Bill Dotson. The illustration appeared as a spread in The AA Grapevine magazine and is seen in AA clubhouses across the world. The original still hangs at Stepping Stones, the home of Bill and Lois Wilson in New York.

Fitzhugh (Fitz) Mayo

The First Success in New York

Fitzhugh Mayo was the first struggling alcoholic Bill W. and Lois brought into their home on Clinton Street in New York and their first New York success. He was a minister's son, a high-society Southerner, and a hopeless drunk. Fitz describes his road from hopelessness to recovery in the Big Book story "Our Southern Friend." He was responsible for bringing AA to the American South and was an important editor of the Big Book.

Early Life and the "Preacher's Kid"

Fitz was born into a prominent family in Virginia. His father was an Episcopal minister. Episcopal churches tended to attract wealthier and more successful Christians. This meant Fitz grew up in a home filled with both faith and high expectations. He was under a lot of pressure to be perfect.

As a young man, Fitz's drinking was a normal part of the social life of a Southern gentleman. But slowly, the social drinking turned into everyday drinking. The alcohol took hold of him.

Fitz's drinking followed the common path of lost jobs, a suffering family, and failing health. By the mid-1930s,

Fitz was desperate. He had been in and out of hospitals and drying out clinics without success.

Meeting Bill Wilson

In 1935 Fitz admitted himself to Towne Hospital in New York. While there, Dr. William Silkworth encouraged Fitz to meet with Bill W. Fitz was skeptical but agreed. AA didn't have a name yet. It was just a small group of people from the Oxford Group trying to stay sober by helping others.

Fitz was a tough case. Because he was a minister's son, he had a religious chip on his shoulder. He was tired of being told to pray his problems away, and felt that if God hadn't helped him yet, God would not help him now.

Bill W. didn't argue with Fitz about religion. Instead, Bill shared his own alcoholic story. He talked about the allergy to alcohol and the mental obsession that made it impossible to stay sober on willpower alone. For the first time, Fitz saw that he wasn't a bad person trying to get good; he was a sick person trying to get well.

Failure, Success, and the Clinton Street Era

After meeting with Bill W., Fitz thought he had learned the philosophy of sobriety, so it was safe for him to return to his home in Maryland. Soon after, he relapsed again. Self-knowledge, willpower, and the security of his family were not enough.

Fitz's sister called Bill W. in New York, despondent over her brother's return to drinking. Bill W. and Lois discussed it and decided to take Fitz into their home. This began the Clinton Street era, the time from 1935 until 1939. During this time, the Brooklyn home of Bill and Lois Wilson served as the unofficial headquarters, sanctuary, and laboratory for the fledgling AA movement.

Fitz Mayo was the first of many struggling alcoholics that Bill and Lois housed, fed, and comforted during that time.

Creating the Big Book

When it came time to write the Big Book, Fitz was part of the small committee that reviewed Bill W.'s chapters.

Fitz was known for being very direct. He and Bill often argued about how the book should talk about God. Fitz, having grown up in a rectory, wanted the book to be more Christian and religious. Others, like Jim Burwell, wanted the book to be more open so that atheists and agnostics could find a way in.

Fitz's passion helped balance the book. He helped ensure that the spiritual foundation of the program was strong. His own story, "Our Southern Friend," became one of the most famous stories in the book.

Carrying the Message to the South

Fitz eventually moved back to Maryland and Virginia. He was one of the first people to bring New York style AA to the southern United States. He lived a life of service until his death in 1943, and he died sober.

Jim Burwell

The Man Who Put God in Italics

Jim Burwell was the militant atheist of early AA. His refusal to believe in a traditional God forced many changes in the text of the Big Book. Because of Jim, the program became open to people of all faiths, or no faith at all.

Early Life and the Start of the Problem

Jim was born in 1898 in a small town in Virginia. His father was a business manager in the Episcopal Church, and Jim grew up with lots of rules and lots of churchgoing. Jim never fit in and thought the people in the church were hypocrites. In his teens, he had become an atheist—someone who does not believe in God.

Jim was a smart, capable young man who worked in sales and, when sober, was good at his job. He started drinking in his teens, and by his twenties, his life was falling apart due to alcohol. He lost jobs, he lost the trust of his family, and ended up living in cheap hotels or on the streets.

Meeting the Group

In 1938, Jim was desperate. He had tried everything to stop drinking, but nothing worked. Family connections put him in touch with a group of men in New York who were staying sober by helping each other. There were about fifteen to twenty of them. It was the group that would one day become Alcoholics Anonymous.

Jim met with Henry Parkhurst and then Bill W. When Jim first met Bill W., he liked what he heard about staying sober, but he hated the God talk. Back then, the movement was closely connected to the Oxford Group. The members talked a lot about Jesus, the Bible, and kneeling in prayer. Jim was loud and stubborn. He told Bill Wilson and the others that he wanted to get sober, but he wouldn't have anything to do with their religious bunk.

Jim Was a Thorn in the Side of the Religious Members

For the first year, Jim was a difficult member. He would sit in meetings and argue with everyone. When they talked about God's will, Jim would talk about group therapy or the power of the team. He stayed sober, but he was angry. Nobody was sure what to do with him. Some thought he should be kicked out.

Bill W. did not want Jim kicked out. Bill realized that if the program required a belief in a specific God, then millions of people who didn't believe would never get help. They would die of alcoholism because they couldn't get past the religious language. Jim was the test case. If the program could work for an atheist like Jim, it could work for anyone.

Jim's Crucial Contributions to the Big Book

When it came time to write the Big Book, Jim was always in the middle of the debates. Bill Wilson wanted to use the word "God" a lot. Jim fought against it. He wanted the book to be more scientific than religious.

A compromise was reached. Instead of just saying "God," the book started using the phrase "God *as we understood Him*." They also added the idea of a Higher Power.

This change meant that God didn't have to be the God of a specific church. A person's Higher Power could be the AA group itself, or nature, or any power greater than ourselves. Jim famously said he liked to think of God as Good Organized Direction. By putting God in a broader context, Jim opened the doors of AA to the world.

Jim's Story: "The Vicious Cycle"

Jim wrote his own story for the first edition of the Big Book, titled "The Vicious Cycle." In it, he is very honest about how bad his drinking was, and his struggle with faith.

Jim came to understand that he had to stop being so militant about his atheism. He saw that his real enemies were his pride and ego. He didn't have to become a religious man, but he did have to become a humble man. He was not the center of the universe.

Later Life and Legacy

Jim Burwell stayed sober for the rest of his life. He moved to Philadelphia and started the first AA group there. He was a great twelfth-stepper, meaning he spent a large amount of time visiting hospitals and jails to help other alcoholics. He was known for being kind, patient, and always willing to tackle the tough cases.

Jim died in 1974 with 36 years of sobriety.

Today, AA is in almost every country in the world. People of all religions—Christians, Jews, Muslims, Hindus, Buddhists—and people who have no religion at all sit in meetings together. They take it for granted that you can choose your own conception of God.

But they wouldn't have that freedom if it wasn't for Jim Burwell. He challenged the founders to be more inclusive and convinced them that the only requirement for membership should be a desire to stop drinking,

Marty Mann

First Woman in AA to Achieve Long-Term Sobriety

Marty Mann was the first woman to find long-term sobriety through the AA program. After finding sobriety inside AA, she spent the rest of her life carrying the message to the world outside AA that alcoholism is a disease, not a moral failing.

Early Life and the Descent into Alcoholism

Marty was born in 1904 into a wealthy and successful family in Chicago. As a young woman, she was social, intelligent, and lived a life of privilege. She traveled to Europe and eventually moved to London, where she became successful in the fashion and magazine industry.

Beneath the surface of her success, a problem was growing. Marty had started drinking. In the beginning, drinking helped her feel confident in social settings. But slowly, the alcohol took control of her. By the 1930s, her life was falling apart. She lost the prestigious job. Her money disappeared, and her health deteriorated.

In those days, society was very cruel to women with drinking problems. Men who drank too much were considered weak, but women who drank were seen as fallen or disgraced. Marty suffered in deep shame. She tried many times to stop on her own, but couldn't. She moved back to the United States and soon found herself in a locked ward of a psychiatric hospital.

Finding Alcoholics Anonymous

In 1939, Marty was a patient at Blythewood Sanitarium in Connecticut. Her doctor was Harry Tiebout. Dr. Tiebout had recently been given a pre-publication copy of a new book called *Alcoholics Anonymous*. He gave it to Marty to read.

At first, Marty was angry. She didn't think she was like the people in the book. She was different. But as she kept reading, she saw herself in the pages.

Marty began attending AA meetings in New York City. AA was tiny, and there were almost no women. Many early members doubted the program would even work for women. Marty proved them wrong. She embraced the Twelve Steps and found a Power greater than herself that could keep her sober.

Her Story in the Big Book

Marty Mann's personal story appears in the second and third editions of the Big Book, titled "Women Suffer Too." In her story, Marty writes honestly about the physical pain and the mental torture of being an alcoholic woman in a world that judged such women harshly.

Thousands of women followed Marty into the program. Before Marty, many women drinkers would stay hidden in their homes, drinking in secret, too afraid to ask for help. Marty's story in the Big Book told them: "You are not alone, and there is a way out."

The National Council on Alcoholism

Marty realized that while AA was wonderful for helping individuals, the public still did not know what alcoholism really was. Most people thought alcoholics were bums who just needed more willpower. Marty wanted that attitude to change.

In 1944, with the encouragement of Bill W., Marty helped start the National Committee for Education on Alcoholism, which later became the National Council on Alcoholism (NCA).

Marty traveled all over the country. She stood in front of crowds and told them she was an alcoholic. This was a shocking thing for a refined woman to say. She campaigned for three main ideas:

1. Alcoholism is a disease.
2. The alcoholic is a sick person who can be helped.
3. Alcoholism is a public health problem and a public responsibility.

Because of Marty's work, hospitals started opening

their doors to alcoholics, and medical schools started teaching doctors about the disease.

A Life of Service

Marty Mann stayed sober for the rest of her life. She faced many challenges, including financial struggles and health issues, but she never returned to drinking. She became one of the most famous women in America, appearing on radio and television to spread her message of hope.

She stayed a close friend to both Bill W. and Lois. She understood that the families of alcoholics needed support too and worked closely with Lois to bring attention to their needs.

A Legacy Beyond AA

Marty passed away in 1980. By the time of her death, the way the world viewed alcoholism had been transformed. She had taken a disgraceful secret and turned it into a public conversation.

Marty Mann was more than just the first woman in AA. She was a bridge between the small, private rooms of AA meetings and the big world outside. When people read "Women Suffer Too" in the Big Book today, they are reading the words of a woman who saved countless lives by refusing to stay silent.

Clarence Snyder

The Man Who Took AA to Cleveland

Clarence Snyder is often called the "Founder of AA in Cleveland." He was a man of high energy, strong opinions, and a deep love for the program that saved his life. While Bill W. and Dr. Bob are the most famous names in this history, Clarence played a huge role in making the fellowship what it is today.

The Early Days

Clarence was born in 1902. Like many who struggled with alcohol, his drinking started out as fun and turned into a nightmare. It destroyed a promising career as a salesman and ruined his marriage. He tried many times to stop on his own, but he always failed.

In early 1938, Clarence was desperate. He had been through several hospitals and cures, all without success. Then he heard about a group of men in Akron, Ohio, who had found a way to stay sober. They were part of the Oxford Group.

He went to Akron to meet Dr. Bob. Clarence was skeptical. He wasn't sure if he liked the religious talk in the Oxford Group. But when he saw the transformation in the men there, he knew he wanted what they had. On February 11, 1938, Clarence had his last drink and became the 40th person to get sober in the Akron group.

Bringing the Message to Cleveland

Clarence lived 35 miles from Akron, in Cleveland. Every week, he would drive to Akron for meetings. Then he started bringing other people from Cleveland with him. By 1939, Clarence felt that there were so many people coming from Cleveland that they should have their own meeting.

This was a big step. Until then, meetings had been held in the homes of members and were closely tied to the Oxford Group. Clarence thought that for the movement to grow, it needed to separate from the heavily religious Oxford Group. He wanted a meeting that focused purely on alcoholism, without the religious requirements.

On May 11, 1939, the first Alcoholics Anonymous meeting was held in Cleveland. It was the first time a group actually used the name Alcoholics Anonymous for their meeting. Clarence pushed for the group to be self-supporting and to focus on the Twelve Steps as they were being written in the Big Book.

Why Cleveland Was Different

Clarence's group in Cleveland was a tremendous success. While the Akron group had remained small, the

Cleveland group grew quickly. Within a year, there were hundreds of members. Part of the success of the Cleveland Group was its emphasis on intensive sponsorship.

In Clarence's view, a sponsor didn't just offer advice. A sponsor was responsible for helping the new person through the Steps quickly. He insisted new members study the Big Book and start working with others right away. This Cleveland Style of sponsorship spread rapidly in Ohio and then across the country.

Naming the Big Book

Clarence also played a key role in naming the movement's basic text. When Bill W. was writing the book, there were many ideas for the title. Bill W. wanted to call it "The Way Out." Others liked "The Frontiers of Freedom."

Clarence pushed hard for the title *Alcoholics Anonymous*. He argued that it perfectly described who the members were and what they did. Because the Cleveland group was already using that name and seeing outstanding success, his opinion carried a lot of weight. In the end, the book—and the entire fellowship—took the name he championed.

The "Home Brewmeister"

Clarence is known for a story in the Big Book called

"The Home Brewmeister." In it, he describes his failed attempts to control his drinking by making his beer at home. It is a classic tale of the insanity of the alcoholic mind—the idea that if a person just changes the type of alcohol or the *way* they drink, they can somehow be normal.

A Life of Service

Clarence remained sober for the rest of his life—over 46 years—and never stopped working with others. Even as Alcoholics Anonymous grew into a worldwide organization, Clarence stayed focused on the old-time; way of doing things. He believed the program should stay simple and that the focus should always be on the Twelve Steps.

He moved to Florida later in life, where he became known for being a tough but fair sponsor to new people. Clarence Snyder passed away in 1984.

Sylvia K.

The First Lady of Chicago

Sylvia K. was known as The First Lady of Chicago, and was one of the first women to find long-term sobriety in AA. Her real name was Sylvia Klause, and after her marriage, Sylvia Latcham. But in AA literature, she has always been referred to as Sylvia K.

At a time when many people thought women could not recover from alcoholism, Sylvia proved them wrong. Her life story, which she titled "The Fearful One" in the second edition of the Big Book, tells the tale of a woman who emerged from deep despair to a life of service and purpose.

Early Problems and the Alcohol Solution

Sylvia was born into a wealthy family in the early 1900s, and was subject to very strict rules for how a lady should act. Although given a life of luxury, she never fit in. For reasons she could not explain, Sylvia was always fearful and nervous.

Alcohol quieted the fear and calmed her. At first, it was a magical solution, that made her feel more social and less anxious. However, as time passed, Sylvia needed more and more of it to get the same feeling. What started as occasional relief from social anxiety turned into a daily necessity.

She married and had children, but her primary relationship was the one she had with the bottle. She tried to stop or control her drinking on her own. She went to hospitals and sought help from doctors, but nothing worked for long.

Finding a New Way

By the late 1930s, Sylvia reached a point of hopelessness. She had lost her marriage and had nowhere left to turn. Then her mother heard about a new group in Akron, Ohio, that was helping people stay sober.

Sylvia traveled to Akron to meet with Dr. Bob. At first, she was skeptical. She had tried everything else, so why would this be different? However, she saw something in the people in Akron she hadn't seen before: people who had been just as hopeless as she was, but who were now happy and sober.

Sylvia spent several weeks in Akron learning the principles of the program. She realized her problem wasn't just about the liquid in the glass; it was about how she dealt with life. She worked the Twelve Steps, focusing on honesty, making amends, and seeking a power greater than herself. For the first time in years, the fear she had carried since childhood lifted.

Bringing the Message to Chicago

When Sylvia returned home, she was the only person in Chicago following this new path. She knew that to stay sober herself, she had to help others, so she looked for alcoholics who wanted to stop drinking.

This was not a simple task. In 1939, there was no central office or phone number for AA. Sylvia worked with a man named Earl T., who had also found sobriety. Together, they visited hospitals and jails and started the first AA group in Chicago with Sylvia's home as a meeting place.

Because she had money, Sylvia could provide more than just emotional support. She helped fund the printing of early AA literature and helped set up a small office. Her social standing helped too. People saw that even a lady from a good family could suffer from this illness—and, more importantly, that she could recover.

The First Lady of Chicago

Sylvia became a mentor to many alcoholic women in the Midwest. She showed them they didn't have to hide in shame. She taught them that sobriety was about more than just not drinking; it was about building a new character and being of use to others.

Sylvia was instrumental in creating the Chicago Intergroup, which helped organize the meetings in the area. She stayed in close contact with Bill W., providing advice and feedback during the writing of the Big Book and the expansion of AA.

Sylvia K. remained sober for the rest of her life. She lived to see Alcoholics Anonymous grow from a handful of people to a worldwide movement. Her story in the Big Book, "The Fearful One," served as a beacon of hope for countless women who felt alone in their struggle. She passed away in 1974.

Part 3: The Spiritual Blueprint

William James

The Will to Believe

William James was a famous American teacher, philosopher, and thinker who died long before the first meeting of Alcoholics Anonymous, but his ideas are found in many places in the Big Book.

A Man Who Studied the Soul

William James was arguably the most talented son in a very talented family. He studied medicine and the human mind, spending his entire life teaching at Harvard University. His younger brother, Henry James, became a novelist and one of the giants of American literature.

From a young age, William struggled with physical and mental problems. He suffered from poor eyesight, back pain, and stomach problems. In his late 20s, William fell into a suicidal depression.

James believed that science had proven that humans were just biological machines and that life was meaningless. He famously wrote about a horrible dread in the pit of his stomach that made him want to give up on life entirely.

He eventually found a way out of the darkness by making a leap of faith. After struggling with the question whether humans have free will, he decided to act as if they did. The idea that people can logically choose to believe things that cannot be scientifically proven is central to much of his work.

The Varieties of Religious Experience

In 1902, James published *The Varieties of Religious Experience*, a book that would exert a great influence on Alcoholics Anonymous. In this book, he looked at hundreds of people who had undergone massive changes because of religious experiences.

He wrote that when people reach rock bottom—when they are completely defeated and have no hope left—they often discover a power greater than themselves to rescue them. He called these events spiritual experiences.

James noticed that these experiences, no matter what religion the person practiced, had three common characteristics. The first was surrender. The person's self-will collapsed, and the person admitted they could not fix themselves. Second, the person would feel a sense of peace and strength that they had never had before. And third, old problems, like an obsession with drink or other destructive behaviors, no longer had power over them.

James's Role in AA History

In 1934, Bill W. was at his lowest point. He was in Towns

Hospital, dying from alcoholism. One night, he had a powerful, white light experience. He felt a spiritual wind and then a sense of peace. Something deep inside him seemed to have changed.

The next morning, Bill worried. He was a man of science and logic, and he feared that the light was just a hallucination caused by belladonna. Belladonna was a drug that he was being given by the doctors as part of what was then called the Towns-Lambert Cure. He discussed his concerns with Dr. Silkworth, his treating physician. The doctor told him it didn't matter what the cause; the experience was real.

A few days later, Bill's friend Ebby Thacher brought him a copy of William James's book, *The Varieties of Religious Experience*. As Bill read it, his fear vanished. His white light experience was exactly like the ones James had described. James's work gave Bill the scientific proof he needed to believe that his experience could signal a true and lasting change.

After Bill Wilson read *The Varieties of Religious Experience* in his hospital bed, he didn't just put it on a shelf and forget about it. He studied it for years. Bill was so impressed by James's work that he made it required reading for early members of the fellowship.

James's Influence on the Big Book

When Bill W. and the early members began writing the Big Book, they used many ideas they learned from the writings of William James.

1. The Educational Variety of Spiritual Experience

In the back of the Big Book, there is an entry called "Spiritual Experience." It explains that not everyone has a white-light moment like Bill W. Most people have what James called the educational variety—a change that happens slowly over time through the Twelve Steps.

2. Utter Hopelessness

James wrote that a person usually has to be completely defeated before they can change. This became Step One. Alcoholics admit they are powerless.

3. Pragmatism (What Works)

William James was a pragmatist. This is a big word that simply means he cared about results. He believed that if a belief improves your life and helps you stay sober, then it can be true for you. This down-to-earth approach is why AA is not a religious program. It doesn't matter how you define God or a Higher Power; what matters is that the definition works for you.

A Lasting Legacy

William James never met Bill W. or Dr. Bob. He never

sat in an AA meeting or drank a cup of basement coffee. Yet, his spirit is in every room where the Big Book is read. He gave the early members of AA the confidence to talk about God and spirituality in a way that made sense to believers and skeptics alike.

Carl Jung

The Doctor Who Saw a Spiritual Solution

Carl Jung was a pioneering Swiss psychiatrist who founded analytical psychology and changed the world by exploring how our deepest mental struggles are tied to our spiritual health. In certain respects, the story of Alcoholics Anonymous began in the quiet offices of Dr. Jung.

A Hopeless Case

In 1931, a wealthy American businessman named Rowland Hazard III went to Switzerland to see Dr. Jung. Rowland was a desperate man. He was a chronic alcoholic who had tried everything to stop drinking: doctors, hospitals, and his own willpower. Nothing worked.

Rowland stayed with Dr. Jung for a year. He thought he was doing well, and that he understood the reasons why he drank. But shortly after leaving Jung's care to come back to the United States, he got drunk again. He returned to Switzerland, feeling defeated and full of despair.

Rowland asked Dr. Jung for the truth: Was there any hope for him? Jung's answer was honest and world-changing. He told Rowland that, as far as medicine and psychology were concerned, his situation was hopeless. There was nothing more science or psychology could do to keep him sober.

The Solution: A Spiritual Experience

Jung did not leave Rowland without hope. He told him that throughout history, certain people in his condition had recovered. But it didn't happen through medicine. It happened through what Jung called a vital spiritual experience.

These experiences were like huge emotional upheavals. A person's old ideas and feelings were cast aside and an entirely new set of values and motives began to dominate their life. Jung admitted that he, as a scientist, didn't know how to produce such an experience for a patient. He suggested Rowland find a religious or spiritual group and hope for a miracle.

From Jung to Bill W.

Rowland took Jung's advice. He joined a group called the Oxford Group, where he eventually had the spiritual experience Jung described. Rowland then passed this message of hope to a friend named Ebby Thacher. Ebby, in turn, brought Jung's message to Bill W. in New York City in 1934.

Bill W. was also a hopeless alcoholic. When Ebby told Bill about his own recovery and the ideas he learned from Rowland (and originally from Dr. Jung), it changed Bill's life. Bill had his own powerful spiritual experience at Towns Hospital.

Jung's Formula for Recovery

Years later, in 1961, Bill W. wrote a letter to Dr. Jung to thank him. He told Jung that his honest conversation with Rowland was the first link in the chain that led to the creation of Alcoholics Anonymous.

Dr. Jung wrote back. In his letter, he explained his view of alcoholism in a way that sounds very much like the AA program. He used a Latin phrase: *Spiritus contra Spiritum.* This means "Spirit against Spirits."

Jung believed the alcoholic's thirst for alcohol was really a hidden thirst for God. He called alcohol the false spirit and God the True Spirit. He believed that humans have a deep, natural hunger for wholeness and a connection to something greater than themselves. Alcohol is a false version of that connection. It makes a person feel at one with the world for a little while, but it ends in destruction.

Jung contributed three important concepts to AA. The first was that alcoholics could not think or understand their way to sobriety. The second was that rather than changing or controlling his habits, the alcoholic needed a deep and vital psychic change. The third was that alcoholics were not bad people; they were people seeking something beautiful but looking in the wrong places.

Carl Jung was a man of science who realized that science has limits. By pointing Rowland Hazard toward a spiritual solution, he opened a door for millions of alcoholics to find a new way of life.

Part 4: Crucial Links in the Chain

Rowland Hazard III

A Pre-AA Success Story

Before there was a Big Book, before there were Steps, and before there were any meetings, there was Rowland Hazard. He never became a member of Alcoholics Anonymous, but he carried the message that the AA way worked before AA even had a name.

A Man of Success and Struggle

Rowland Hazard III was born in 1881 into a very wealthy and respected family in Rhode Island. His family owned many businesses and was well known in their community. Rowland graduated from Yale University, after which he became a successful businessman and then a state senator.

But Rowland was an alcoholic. Rowland tried everything he could to stop drinking. Nothing worked. No matter how much he wanted to stay sober, he always returned to the bottle.

Searching for a Cure in Switzerland

By the early 1930s, Rowland's drinking had become life-threatening. His family was desperate. They sent him to Switzerland to see Dr. Carl Jung, one of the most famous psychiatrists in the world. If anyone could fix Rowland's mind, the family believed it was him.

Rowland stayed in Switzerland and worked with Dr. Jung for about a year. While there, he stayed sober and learned about the workings of his mind. He came to believe that he understood himself well enough to never drink again.

However, shortly after leaving Dr. Jung's care, Rowland drank. The old patterns returned immediately. He was devastated. He returned to Dr. Jung a total failure and asked what had gone wrong.

The Great Physician's Verdict

Dr. Jung was honest with him. He told Rowland that he was a chronic alcoholic. He explained that in all his years of medicine, he had never seen a person in Rowland's condition recover through medical or psychological means alone.

Rowland was shocked. He asked if there was any hope at all. Dr. Jung told him there was one exception. Occasionally, throughout history, certain people had what he called huge emotional displacements and spiritual rearrangements. We call these spiritual experiences. Dr. Jung told Rowland that unless he could have one of those, he was doomed to die or go insane from his drinking.

This was The Great Verdict. It stripped Rowland of his last bit of pride. He realized that human power—even the power of the world's best doctor—could not save him.

Finding the Solution

Rowland went back to the United States and joined the Oxford Group. The Oxford Group was not for alcoholics specifically; it was a Christian movement that practiced honesty, unselfishness, and helpfulness to others. The members believed in turning one's life over to God and making amends for past wrongs.

Rowland found the spiritual connection in the Oxford Group that Dr. Jung had described. He stopped relying on his own strength and started relying on a Power greater than himself. To his amazement, the urge to drink left him. He was sober, and for the first time in years, he stayed sober.

Passing it On

The Oxford Group had a pass it on program called Life Changing. The group considered themselves and others to be sin sick due to pride, selfishness, and fear. A member's duty was to help other sin-sick people by Personal Witnessing. That meant telling their own story and how they became well by following God's will. To the Oxford Group, alcoholism was only a symptom of being sin sick.

According to the tenets of the Oxford Group, to keep what he had, Roland had to give it away. Because his most serious problem was alcoholism, he went looking for other alcoholics to hear his personal testimony.

In 1934, Rowland heard about an old school friend named Ebby Thacher. Ebby was a heavy drinker who was about to be locked up in an institution. Rowland and two other friends from the Oxford Group intervened in the court proceedings, asking that Ebby be released to them rather than be sent to jail or a mental institution. The judge agreed.

Rowland and his friends shared their stories and told Ebby about the spiritual solution. Because Rowland was someone who knew alcoholism, Ebby listened.

Ebby got sober, and a few months later, Ebby went to visit his old friend Bill Wilson. Ebby sat across from Bill at a kitchen table and told him, "I've got religion." Bill was skeptical at first, but when he saw the change in Ebby, he couldn't ignore it. Ebby told Bill what Rowland had learned from Dr. Jung: that the only hope for a chronic alcoholic was a spiritual experience.

Return to Ordinary Life

Rowland Hazard didn't become a famous leader in AA. After helping Ebby, he continued his life as a businessman and a family man. Nevertheless, he was a crucial link in the chain of events that brought the ideas of Dr. Jung to the streets of New York. The story of the certain American businessman in Chapter 2 is

Rowland's story. The conversation with Dr. Jung described in "There is a Solution" is his conversation.

He passed away in 1945, the same year AA was celebrating its tenth anniversary.

Ebby Thacher

The Man Who Brought the Message to Bill W.

One of the most famous and dramatic scenes in the Big Book is Bill W.'s description of his meeting with his old drinking buddy Ebby. Bill was living the life of a late-stage alcoholic. Ebby was sober and healthy. When asked what happened, Ebby said he didn't drink anymore. He got religion.

Ebby's Youth and Early Drinking

Edwin Thacher, whom everyone called Ebby, was born in 1896 into a wealthy family in Albany, New York. His father had been the mayor of Albany and a judge.

Ebby met Bill Wilson when they were both students at a prestigious private school called Burr and Burton Academy, nestled in the Green Mountains of Vermont. Bill was a star at the school, excelling at everything. Ebby was a scamp, more interested in fun and pranks than his studies. Nevertheless, the two of them became fast friends.

Bill and Ebby had one thing in common: a growing problem with alcohol. In those early days, drinking was part of their social life. Later it would take over their lives.

As Ebby grew older, drinking became a necessity, and his family's money couldn't protect him from the consequences. He lost jobs, he lost the respect of his community, and he lost his health. By the early 1930s, Ebby was a hopeless drunk.

The Turning Point

In 1934, Ebby's drinking had become so bad that he faced being sent to jail or an institution. He had been arrested for several alcohol-related crimes, including drunkenly driving a car into a neighbor's kitchen.

While he was waiting in court for sentencing, three men from the Oxford Group appeared in the courtroom and asked to be heard. One of those men was Rowland Hazard. These men told the judge they had found a way to stay sober through spiritual means and asked that Ebby be released to them. After the judge agreed, they then told Ebby about their own experiences and how they had found a way to stop drinking through spiritual principles.

Ebby decided to give it a try. He lived with Rowland for a while and stayed sober. Later he moved into the Calvary Mission in New York City to start his life over. When being honest about his faults and trying to help other people, he found he no longer had the desire to drink.

Carrying the Message to Bill W.

As Ebby was getting sober, Bill W. was living in Brooklyn, drinking heavily, and losing hope. After many hospitalizations for alcoholism, Bill was afraid he was going to die or go crazy.

In November 1934, Ebby went to Bill's house. According to the Big Book, Bill was sitting at his kitchen table with a bottle of gin, expecting his old friend to join him for a drink. But Ebby refused. He looked healthy; his eyes were clear, and he seemed different. When Bill asked him what happened, Ebby simply said, "I've got religion."

Bill was surprised and a little skeptical. He didn't like the idea of religion. But Ebby explained it in a way that Bill could understand. Ebby told him, "Why don't you choose your own conception of God?" This one idea changed everything for Bill. It meant he didn't have to follow a specific church or set of rules; he just had to be willing to believe in a Power greater than himself.

In later years, Lois suggested that the story of the meeting published in the Big Book had been polished by Bill for dramatic effect. According to her, Ebby visited several times over a period of weeks and was often less than the clear-eyed messenger that is described in the Big Book.

Whatever the details of the meeting, Bill continued to

drink for several weeks after talking with Ebby, but his next hospitalization would be his final one. While he was in the hospital bed, he had a powerful spiritual experience and realized that Ebby was right.

A Life of Ups and Downs

Ebby Thacher is sometimes considered the original messenger of AA. He showed that one alcoholic could help another when no one else could. However, Ebby's own journey was not easy.

While Bill Wilson and Dr. Bob went on to build a worldwide movement, Ebby struggled. For many years, he went in and out of sobriety. He had long periods of sobriety and helped many people, but he had many relapses into drinking.

Despite his slips, the AA community never gave up on him.

Bill Wilson remained Ebby's friend for the rest of his life. Bill often sent Ebby money and made sure he had a place to stay. He never forgot the debt he owed to the man who came to his home and offered him a way out of the darkness.

Ebby's Legacy

Ebby Thacher is a central figure in the literature of Alcoholics Anonymous. A person can find his influence in several places. Much of the first chapter of the Big

Book, "Bill's Story," is about Bill's interaction with Ebby. Although Bill refers to him only as a friend to protect his privacy, everyone in the early days knew it was Ebby. Ebby showed Bill the power of one alcoholic talking to another. And Ebby tells Bill that he can choose his own conception of God. This would become a fundamental part of Alcoholics Anonymous.

Ebby Thacher spent the last years of his life in a quiet town in New York, supported by the friends he had made in the program and the kindness of Bill Wilson. He died in 1966, having been sober for over two years.

Henrietta Seiberling

The Woman Who Connected Bill W. and Dr. Bob

Henrietta Seiberling was at the right place at the right time, and because of it, became a crucial link in the chain of events that led to the creation of Alcoholics Anonymous. She was a woman of faith and a member of the Akron Oxford Group. When Bill W. found himself in Akron, feeling like drinking and looking for another drunk to talk to, he was directed to Henrietta for help. What followed was one of the most important meetings in all of AA history.

A Life of Privilege and Challenge

Henrietta Buckler was born in 1888 into the upper crust of society in Akron, Ohio. She married John Seiberling. John was the son of the man who started the Goodyear Tire and Rubber Company in Akron. After their marriage, they lived in a home on his parents massive estate.

However, money and status did not protect Henrietta from misfortune. Her marriage was unhappy because of her husband's infidelity, but divorce was not an option. To avoid scandal, his family orchestrated a compromise whereby their son moved back into the main mansion with his parents and she stayed in the house on the estate where she had raised her children. That house was a small stone building called Gate Lodge. She lived there with her children. It was a lonely existence. Hoping to find a solution to her loneliness, she joined the Akron Oxford Group.

Henrietta found the relief she was looking for in the ideas of the Oxford Group and had the freedom to host the group at her home. She became the leader of the Akron group.

Meeting Dr. Bob

One of the people Henrietta wanted to help was a local doctor named Robert Smith—the man we now know as Dr. Bob. Dr. Bob was a well-respected surgeon, but he had a secret: he was an alcoholic. She learned of him because Dr. Bob's wife, Anne, had brought Bob to meetings of the Akron Oxford Group held at Gate Lodge.

Henrietta knew that Dr. Bob was a good man suffering from a terrible sickness. She prayed for a way to help him, and believed that if Dr. Bob could just talk to someone who truly understood his problem, he might find a way out.

The Famous Phone Call

On Mother's Day in May 1935, Bill W. was in Akron on a business trip. He was sober, something he had accomplished by talking to other alcoholics, but was away from home and on shaky ground.

Bill's business deal in Akron failed. He was alone in the Mayflower Hotel, feeling depressed and tempted to go into the bar. He knew that if he took one drink, he would be lost. Bill needed to find another alcoholic to help.

Bill went to a church directory in the hotel lobby and started making phone calls. He eventually reached a member of the Oxford Group who gave him Henrietta Seiberling's phone number. He told her, "I'm an alcoholic from New York, and I need to find another alcoholic to talk to so I can stay sober."

This was the answer to Henrietta's prayers. She invited Bill to her home at the Gate Lodge.

The Meeting at the Gate Lodge

When Bill arrived, Henrietta listened to his story. She was impressed by his honesty and his desire to help others. She then called Anne Smith and told her she had found someone who could help with Dr. Bob.

At first, Dr. Bob didn't want to go. He was tired and hungover. He told his wife he would stay for fifteen minutes. But when Bill and Bob started talking in Henrietta's small library, something happened. Because Bill spoke about his own failures and his own struggle with drink, Dr. Bob didn't feel judged. He felt understood.

The fifteen-minute meeting lasted for hours. Henrietta and Anne stayed in the background, making sure the two men had what they needed and offering their support. Henrietta was witness to what some consider the first meeting of Alcoholics Anonymous. It was Bill putting into practice for the first time the system of one drunk talking to another.

After that meeting, Henrietta remained a close friend and advisor to the early members of AA. She helped them understand the spiritual principles of the Oxford Group, principles that Bill would later transform into the Twelve Steps. She also helped Bill and Bob stay focused on the idea of one alcoholic helping another.

Henrietta's Later Criticisms of AA

As AA moved away from the Oxford Group, Henrietta became one of AA's most vocal critics. Henrietta was convinced that the success of the Oxford Group was due solely to God's power, and that AA, by focusing on alcoholism, was becoming too human and professional. She famously said, "We're not out to please the alcoholics. They have been pleasing themselves all these years. We are out to please God."

Henrietta thought that by embracing ideas from Carl Jung and William James, AA was becoming too psychological, and she was deeply suspicious of the efforts to raise money to print the Big Book. "Money will spoil everything," she warned.

Henrietta never wanted AA to become its own separate organization. She loved the discipline of the Oxford Group and felt that when the alcoholic squad broke away to form AA, they lost the spiritual anchor that kept them honest. Despite the differences, she remained close to Bill and Bob until her death.

Later in life, Henrietta moved to New York, where she worked next to Lois, Bill's wife, and became the first paid member of Al-anon. Henrietta Seiberling passed away in 1979 at the age of 91.

The Oxford Group

AA's Spiritual Parent

What was the Oxford Group?

Before there was Alcoholics Anonymous, there was the Oxford Group. It was not a group for alcoholics. It was a Christian fellowship founded by an American minister named Frank Buchman in the early 1900s. Buchman believed that the world's problems resulted from personal problems. He thought that if individuals changed their lives and followed God's will, the world would change for the better.

The Oxford Group was not a typical church. It did not have official members, a specific building, or a set of strict rules. Instead, the movement focused on a way of living. It became very popular in the 1920s and 1930s by encouraging people to return to what they called First-Century Christian Fellowship. This meant living simply and honestly, just like the very first followers of Jesus. Rather than following a list of dos and don'ts, followers of the Oxford Group tried to listen for God's guidance in their daily lives.

The Four Absolutes and the Five Procedures

To help people change, the Oxford Group followed two main sets of guidelines. These guides later became the foundation for the Twelve Steps of AA.

The first set was called the Four Absolutes. These were the goals every person should strive for:

- Absolute Honesty: No lying to yourself or others.
- Absolute Purity: Having clean thoughts and actions.
- Absolute Unselfishness: Helping others without wanting anything in return.
- Absolute Love: Caring for everyone, even your enemies.

The second set was the Five Procedures. This was how they practiced their faith:

- Giving in to God (surrender).
- Listening for God's guidance (quiet time).
- Checking that guidance against the Four Absolutes.
- Sharing your sins with another person (confession).
- Making up for the wrongs you did to others (restitution).

The New York Connection: Bill Wilson's Start

Bill Wilson lived in Brooklyn, and his office was in Manhattan. He was very familiar with the Calvary Episcopal Church, which was the American headquarters for the Oxford Group. He had seen the well-dressed members of the group and had likely heard of their house parties and their leader, Sam Shoemaker.

However, to a cynical, scientifically-minded stockbroker like Bill, the Oxford Group was a club for people who didn't have real problems. He didn't think their quiet times and prayers could do anything for a man who was dying of alcoholism. He famously said that he had no use for religion and thought it was for people who weren't strong enough to handle life on their own.

Not until Bill's old friend Ebby came to see him and explained how the Oxford Group had helped him overcome drinking, did Bill consider the possibility that the Oxford Group held a solution for him.

The Akron Connection: Dr. Bob and Henrietta Seiberling

Henrietta Seiberling was a leader in the Akron Oxford Group and hosted meetings in her home. She was particularly worried about a local surgeon named Dr. Bob Smith, who was an alcoholic.

When Bill W. showed up in Akron on business, looking for another alcoholic to talk to, he located Henrietta, and she directed him to Dr. Bob. The rest is history.

Differences Between New York and Akron

Even though the Oxford Group functioned in both New York and Akron, they operated differently.

1. Focus and Size:

In New York, the Oxford Group was massive and focused on Changing the World through Personal Evangelism. It felt like a big movement. In Akron, the group was much smaller and more focused on the local community. It felt more like a support group for families.

2. The Role of Alcoholics:

In New York, Bill Wilson and the other alcoholics felt like they were a side project for the Oxford Group. The leaders of the group wanted Bill to focus on bringing in famous and powerful people, but Bill only wanted to help other drunks. This caused a lot of tension. In Akron, the alcoholics were more integrated into the group, but they still kept their identity as a squad within the larger fellowship.

3. Simplicity vs. Complexity:

Bill Wilson in New York liked to write and organize. He eventually wrote the Big Book to explain the AA method. Dr. Bob in Akron preferred to keep things simple and oral. He often said that the Four Absolutes and the Bible were all they really needed.

4. The Break from the Group:

By 1937, the New York alcoholics left the Oxford Group to create a path just for alcoholics that was spiritual but not religious so that even atheists could join.

In Akron, Dr. Bob remained loyal to the Christian roots of the group. The Akron alcoholics stayed with the

Oxford Group until 1939, the year the Big Book was published.

The Legacy of the Oxford Group for Alcoholics Anonymous

In the end, the alcoholics in both cities realized they needed their own identity. They took the best parts of the Oxford Group—the honesty, the making of amends, the spiritual surrender, and the helping of others—and turned them into the Twelve Steps.

The Oxford Group provided the tools, but Alcoholics Anonymous provided the community. Without the Oxford Group, Bill Wilson and Dr. Bob might never have found the principles that saved their lives, but they eventually realized that the strict religiosity of the Oxford Group would not work for alcoholics.

Part 5: The Healing Friends (Medical & Spiritual Support)

Dr. William Duncan Silkworth

The Doctor Who Found the Phenomenon of Craving

The early members of AA called Dr. Silkworth "the little doctor who loved drunks." When the world looked upon alcoholics as bad people or moral failures, Dr. Silkworth saw them as sick people who needed help. He is the author of "The Doctor's Opinion" which, after the prefaces, begins the Big Book.

A Different Way of Looking at Drinking

Dr. Silkworth was born in 1873. He became a medical doctor and eventually went to work at Towns Hospital in New York City. Towns Hospital was a place where wealthy alcoholics went to dry out.

In the 1930s, most doctors thought alcoholism was just a lack of willpower. They believed that if a person really wanted to stop, they could. It wasn't that people couldn't stop; they just wouldn't. If self-destruction was their choice, then they belonged in either an institution or in jail.

Dr. Silkworth saw something different. He worked with thousands of alcoholics and realized that for an alcoholic, drinking wasn't just a bad habit. It was a physical and mental problem that the person could not control on their own.

The Theory of the Allergy

Dr. Silkworth called alcoholism an allergy.

When we think of an allergy today, we think of someone who breaks out in a rash if they eat a peanut or get a sting from a bee. Dr. Silkworth used the word allergy to explain that the alcoholic's body, when it ingested alcohol, produced the phenomenon of craving.

He explained it like this: Most people can have a drink or two and stop. Their bodies handle the alcohol normally. But for the alcoholic, one drink triggers a physical craving for more. Their bodies react differently than other people's bodies. Once they take that first drink, they lose control over how much they drink.

Along with this physical allergy, there was a mental obsession. This meant that even when the alcoholic was sober and knew that drinking would lead to ruin, their mind would talk them into taking that first drink again.

This was a monumental discovery. It told the alcoholic, "You aren't a bad person trying to become better. You are a sick person trying to get well."

Meeting Bill W.

In 1934, Bill Wilson was admitted to Towns Hospital for the fourth time due to alcoholism. Dr. Silkworth liked Bill, but he was honest with Bill's wife, Lois. He told her that Bill would likely die or have to be locked up forever because his brain was being destroyed by drink.

Dr. Silkworth explained his theory of the physical allergy and the mental obsession to Bill. For the first time, Bill understood *why* he couldn't stop. He wasn't just weak; he was sick.

When Bill later had a spiritual experience that removed his urge to drink, he went back to Dr. Silkworth. Bill was afraid he was going crazy. Dr. Silkworth listened to Bill's story and told him, "Whatever you have, hang on to it. It is much better than what you had before."

Dr. Silkworth encouraged Bill to share what had happened to him with other alcoholics. He told Bill not to preach, but to tell them the hard medical facts about the allergy and the obsession. Once a person realized they were physically hopeless, they would be much more willing to look for a spiritual solution.

The "Doctor's Opinion"

When it came time to write the Big Book in 1939, Bill Wilson needed the support of the medical world. He asked Dr. Silkworth to write a letter for the beginning of the book.

It was a big risk for a doctor to put his name on a book about a spiritual group. It could have ruined his reputation. But Dr. Silkworth believed in what these men were doing. He wrote what we now call "The Doctor's Opinion."

Dr. Silkworth's letter gave AA medical credibility. He stated clearly that he believed the AA program was the only thing he had seen work for hopeless alcoholics.

A Life of Service

Dr. Silkworth worked with alcoholics his whole life. He became the director of the Knickerbocker Hospital in New York, where he set up a special ward for alcoholics.

He never gave up on anyone. Even when a person relapsed dozens of times, "Silky," as they called him, was always there with a smile and an encouraging word. He estimated that he treated more than 40,000 alcoholics in his career.

In his final years, Dr. Silkworth was quite frail, but he refused to slow down. Bill W. and some other early AA members worried about him because he wasn't making much money and his health was failing. In 1950, they tried to raise money to help retire to a farm in New Hampshire. However, he died of a heart attack in 1951, at the age of 77, before he could move to that farm.

Bill W. famously said that the doctor died with his boots on, meaning he was still working and helping patients right until his last day. After he passed away, the AA community was so grateful for his service that they raised a large sum of money to help support his widow, Marie.

Dr. Harry Tiebout

The Psychiatrist Who Understood Surrender

In the early days of Alcoholics Anonymous, most doctors and psychiatrists did not know how to help alcoholics. They saw alcoholism as a sign of a weak mind. Dr. Harry Tiebout was different. He was one of the first medical professionals to see that AA worked and spent much of his life explaining it to the rest of the medical world.

Who Was Harry Tiebout?

Harry Tiebout was born in 1899. He became a psychiatrist, and in the late 1930s, he was working at the posh Blythewood Sanitarium in Connecticut,

In the 1930s and 40s, most psychiatrists followed Sigmund Freud. They believed that if you could just figure out your hidden childhood problems, you would stop drinking. Dr. Tiebout tried this with his alcoholic patients, but he noticed a big problem: his patients would understand why they drank, but they still couldn't stop drinking.

The Turning Point: Marty Mann

In 1939, Dr. Tiebout was treating a patient named Marty Mann. Marty was a very sick alcoholic. Everything Dr. Tiebout tried had failed.

One day, Bill Wilson gave Dr. Tiebout a manuscript of the Big Book, which was about to be published. Dr. Tiebout gave it to Marty to read. At first, Marty was put off by all the talk of God, but she stuck with it. As she continued reading, she saw herself in the stories and realized that she was not alone.

Marty had a powerful spiritual experience and got sober. Dr. Tiebout felt that he'd witnessed a miracle. He'd watched a woman who was hopeless suddenly become well. He decided to study Marty and the AA program to understand the science behind her change.

The doctor was so impressed with the draft of the Big Book, he sought out the author. Bill W. and Dr. Tiebout became lifelong friends.

The Ego and the Pink Cloud

Dr. Tiebout is best known for his ideas about the ego. He believed Freud was wrong about alcoholics. Alcoholics didn't need more ego or more self-knowledge. Instead, they had inflated egos. This didn't mean they thought they were better than everyone; it meant that to feel okay, they had to be in control of everything. That is they struggled to listen to the ideas of others or admit it when they were wrong.

The only way for an alcoholic to get better was to surrender that ego. This discovery made the doctor a firm supporter of the 12 Steps. He saw that AA. was doing something medicine couldn't: it was teaching people how to be humble.

He observed that when an alcoholic is drinking, their ego is puffed up. They think they can handle their liquor, that it isn't a problem, or that they can fix their lives on their own. This was the defiance of the alcoholic.

He also coined the term pink cloud. He noticed that when people first get sober in AA, they often feel incredibly happy and wonderful. While this is good, he warned it can be dangerous. They might start thinking, "I've got this handled now. I don't need meetings anymore." Dr. Tiebout taught that true recovery requires ongoing efforts to stay humble.

Surrender vs. Submission

Dr. Tiebout pointed out an important difference between submission and surrender.

Submission is when you give up because you have to, but you remain angry inside. It's found in a person who stops drinking because their spouse threatens to leave them. They aren't drinking, but they are still fighting the idea of being an alcoholic. Their ego is still in charge, just waiting for a chance to drink again.

Surrender is different. Surrender is when a person truly accepts that they are powerless over alcohol. They stop fighting. They stop making excuses. When a person surrenders, they stop trying to run the show.

Dr. Tiebout told the medical world that AA was successful because it helped people reach this state of surrender.

A Bridge Between Two Worlds

For many years, doctors and AA members didn't trust each other. AA members thought doctors were too cold and clinical. Doctors thought AA was a religious cult.

Dr. Tiebout acted as a bridge. Because he was a respected psychiatrist, other doctors listened to him. He wrote papers for medical journals explaining that AA was a valid treatment for alcoholism. He told his colleagues, they should not be jealous of AA. They should learn from it.

By the late 1940s, Bill Wilson had been sober for over a decade, but he was miserable. He was suffering from deep depression. He couldn't understand why he was so unhappy, even though he wasn't drinking.

Dr. Tiebout explained to Bill that he was suffering from an unreduced ego. Even though Bill had stopped drinking, his emotions were pushing him to act like a drinker. He was still demanding that everything in life go his way, and when it didn't, he collapsed into despair.

Tiebout taught Bill that staying away from a bottle is just the first step. The real goal is emotional sobriety. This means learning how to be okay even when things go wrong. It means not letting your happiness depend on other people or outside events. Bill took these medical ideas and turned them into a famous essay in the Grapevine, called "The Next Frontier: Emotional Sobriety."

His Legacy

While Dr. Tiebout did not write the Big Book, his ideas are woven into the way we talk about recovery today. When we talk about hitting bottom, we are talking about the moment of surrender that Tiebout described. When we talk about self-will run riot, we are talking about the inflated ego that Tiebout warned us about.

In 1951, Dr. Tiebout was a key speaker at the AA International Convention. He helped the fellowship celebrate its 15th anniversary. He remained a Class A (nonalcoholic) trustee of the General Service Board for many years.

The Final Years

Dr. Harry Tiebout passed away in 1966. He never

claimed to be an alcoholic, but he had the humility to realize that the alcoholics in AA had found a truth that he hadn't found in his medical books.

He taught us that recovery isn't just about stopping the use of a substance. It is about a change of heart. It is about moving from a life of "I can do it myself" to a life of "I need help." By combining the science of the mind with the spirit of the 12 Steps, Dr. Tiebout built a foundation whereby the medical community would support AA for generations to come.

Sister Ignatia

The Angel of Alcoholics Anonymous

Sister Ignatia was a small woman with a giant heart. She played a huge part in the early days of Alcoholics Anonymous. She has been called the third founder and the Angel of AA.

Her Early Life

Sister Ignatia was born Della Mary Gavin in Ireland in 1889. When she was young, her family moved to the United States and settled in Cleveland, Ohio. When she was twenty-five years old, she dedicated her life to God by joining the Sisters of Charity of St. Augustine. She took the name Sister Mary Ignatia.

Sister Ignatia spent 20 years as a music teacher. While that may sound like a peaceful job, for her it was not. She was a perfectionist and worked herself to the bone to make sure every student played at the highest level and every performance was flawless.

By 1933, the strain became too much. She wasn't just tired; she suffered what doctors back then called nervous exhaustion (today we might call it a total burnout or a breakdown). She became physically ill and couldn't handle the noise, the pressure of the students, or the long hours.

Her superiors in the Sisters of Charity realized she could no longer teach. They transferred her to St. Thomas Hospital in Akron, Ohio, to do light work. They put her in the front office, signing people in. She considered it a demotion, and her life's work a failure.

Sister Ignatia did admissions at the front desk in the same hospital where Dr. Bob was practicing medicine.

A Meeting of Minds

St. Thomas was a Catholic hospital, and in the 1930s, alcoholics could not be admitted as patients. The hospital and most doctors saw drunks as nuisances who took up beds from truly sick people.

At the front desk, Sister Ignatia often had to turn away desperate people. One night, a man was brought in suffering from drunken jitters. Instead of turning him away, she snuck him into a small room called the Flower Room. It was a room used to store floral arrangements for patients who had passed away.

She needed a doctor who wouldn't judge the man or report her for breaking the rules. She knew Dr. Bob Smith worked at the hospital and had heard rumors that he understood these kinds of patients. When she approached him, she found him to be just as compassionate as she was. Together, they formed a secret team. Dr. Bob provided the medical care, and Sister Ignatia provided the sanctuary.

This Flower Room became the very first detox unit for AA members. Sister Ignatia and Dr. Bob worked together to help the patient through the physical pain of stopping alcohol, and then guided them to the spiritual long-term solution.

How She Helped the Early Members

Sister Ignatia was kind and gentle, but she was also firm. She expected the patients to be honest and to work hard on their recovery.

She did three things that became famous in AA history:

1. **The Sacred Heart Badge:** When a person was ready to leave the hospital after five days of treatment, Sister Ignatia would give them a small religious medal. She would make them promise that if they ever felt like taking a drink again, they would return the medal to her first. This gave the person a reason to pause and think before picking up a drink.
2. **The Importance of Coffee:** She was one of the first people to realize that alcoholics needed a place to talk and feel safe. She made sure there was always plenty of hot coffee and a safe place for conversation. Thus, began the coffee culture that is still a big part of AA meetings today.
3. **Dignity and Love:** Most of all, she treated every person as important. She didn't look down on them because of their past. She saw the real person underneath the alcohol.

Her Struggles

Sister Ignatia was a saintly woman, but she was also human. She worked very long hours and often neglected her own rest. She sometimes struggled with her own health because she gave so much of herself to others.

Her superiors in her church were not always supportive of her work, and some in the community thought it was scandalous for a nun to be spending so much time with drunks. But Sister Ignatia stayed true to what she believed. She once said that she saw the face of Christ in every suffering alcoholic who walked through her door.

The Later Years

After many years in Akron, Sister Ignatia was moved to Cleveland to start Rosary Hall Solarium at St. Vincent Charity Hospital. This was a dedicated wing just for treating alcoholics. It was beautiful and bright, designed to make people feel like they were in a home rather than a prison.

Even as she grew older and her health declined, she continued to visit patients. Thousands of people credited her with saving their lives.

Her Legacy

Sister Ignatia passed away in 1966 at the age of 77. At

her funeral, thousands of people attended. Many of them were alcoholics she had treated in the Flower Room and Rosary Hall.

The five-day detox model she helped create became a standard for hospitals everywhere. Bill and Bob gave AA the program and the Big Book. Sister Ignatia gave AA its coffee pots and its conversations that last into the night.

Reverend Samuel Shoemaker

The Man Who Helped Shape AA

Reverend Samuel Shoemaker was a minister and a leader who believed that spiritual principles could change any person's life. Sam Shoemaker's influence on AA was so huge that Bill W. once said, "It was from Sam Shoemaker that most of AA's spiritual principles came."

A Man with a Mission

Sam Shoemaker was born in 1893. He became a minister in the Episcopal Church and the senior pastor of Calvary Church in New York City, a wealthy and influential church. But Sam was not a man willing to live inside a church. He wanted to help people where they lived and suffered.

Reverend Shoemaker believed the traditional church had become stale and boring. He felt that most Christians were just going through the motions on Sundays without changing their lives.

When he met Frank Buchman, the founder of the Oxford Group, in China in 1918, Sam had a spiritual awakening. He decided that the church shouldn't be a place for rituals; it should be a place for life-changing action.

Back in New York, Sam was worried that regular people—especially those struggling with things like alcoholism—didn't feel welcome in fancy churches. So he made Calvary the headquarters for the Oxford Group and turned his church into a hub where people who had given up on religion could find a simple, practical way to connect with God.

Ebby, Bill, and the Calvary Rescue Mission

One of the men who came to Sam's church was Ebby Thacher. Ebby got sober in Vermont but moved to New York to be close to the heart of the Oxford Movement. When he went to meet Bill W., Ebby was living at the Calvary Rescue Mission. A condition of living there was that he pass the message on to others. One of the others Ebby chose was his old friend Bill W.

After Ebby's visit, Bill was curious. A few nights later, Bill went to see where Ebby was staying. Bill stumbled into the Calvary Rescue Mission high as a kite with a bottle of gin in his pocket. When he arrived, the mission was full of homeless men eating a dinner of beef stew and beans. Bill, trying to be friendly, stood up and gave a rambling, drunken speech about how he was one of them and that he had found a new way to live.

The men at the mission thought Bill was a joke. But

Ebby didn't give up on him. He took Bill into the back, fed him, and listened to him. This embarrassing visit was the final nudge Bill needed. A few days later, he checked himself into Towns Hospital for the last time.

Sam and the Alcoholic Squad

The Oxford Group liked to organize people into specialized teams or squads based on their background. For example, they had squads for businessmen, squads for students, and squads for society women. Both in Akron and in New York, there was an alcoholic squad.

Sam allowed the drunk squad of the Oxford Group to meet at Calvary House,a building right next to his church. It gave them a place to feel safe.

Helping Write the Big Book

When it came time for Bill W. to write the Big Book, he turned to Sam Shoemaker for advice. Sam was a very talented writer. Bill wanted to make sure the book was clear and that the spiritual ideas were solid.

Many of the Twelve Steps are based on things Sam taught. The ideas of self examination (Step 4), confession (Step 5), restitution (Step 9), and prayer and meditation (Step 11) were all core parts of Sam's teaching in the Oxford Group.

Bill W. once suggested that Sam write the Twelve Steps. Sam declined. He told Bill that the Steps should be written by an alcoholic for other alcoholics.

A Bridge Between Religion and AA

In the early days, there was a lot of tension between organized religion and the new groups of alcoholics. Some people thought AA was a cult, and some alcoholics were afraid of the church. Sam Shoemaker acted as a peacemaker between the two groups.

He explained to the public that AA was not replacing the church. Instead, it was a way for people who were lost to find a spiritual path. He defended AA to other ministers, telling them that these drunks were often doing a better job of living out spiritual truths than the people sitting in the pews.

In the 1940s, Sam walked away from the Oxford Group, an organization he had helped lead for nearly twenty years. He left because of a dispute with Frank Buchman the founder of the Oxford Group, over Frank's desire to take the group in a more political direction. Sam, however, continued his connection to AA. He spoke at AA conventions and wrote articles for the Grapevine.

His Character and Legacy

Those who knew Sam Shoemaker described him as a man of great energy and warmth. He had a way of looking at a person and making them feel as if they mattered. He was a human minister who was honest about his own struggles with fear and selfishness.

In his final years, Sam lived in Pittsburgh and led a massive spiritual movement there called the Pittsburgh Experiment, which encouraged people to try God in their daily lives, much like he had encouraged the early members of AA to do. He died in 1963.

Father Edward Dowling

The Jesuit Friend of AA

Few non-alcoholics knew the heart of an alcoholic better than Father Edward Dowling. Known simply as Father Ed to many early members of Alcoholics Anonymous, this Jesuit priest from St. Louis played a huge role in the spiritual growth of the movement.

Who Was Father Ed?

Edward Dowling was born in 1898. A natural-born storyteller, before becoming a priest he worked as a reporter. He loved the fast-paced life of a city reporter, covering crime, politics, and the daily struggles of people in St. Louis. However, he felt a spiritual itch.

As a reporter, his job was to stand on the sidelines and watch people's lives fall apart so he could write a story about it. He began to feel that his true calling wasn't to describe the world's problems, but to do something about them.

In 1919, he left the newspaper and joined the Jesuits (The Society of Jesus). The Jesuits are the intellectual soldiers of the Catholic Church. They are teachers, thinkers, and activists. This was the perfect fit for Ed because he could keep his sharp newsman brain but use it to help people find spiritual solutions to their problems.

As a Jesuit priest, he was active in social causes. He fought for fair housing, better labor rights, and racial equality. Because of his own struggles with health—especially arthritis, which caused him constant pain—he understood what it was to live with a problem that you could not fix on your own. He called his physical disability his thorn in the flesh.

A Cold Night in New York

One rainy, cold night in November 1940, Bill Wilson was in the middle of a pity party. He was struggling with depression and felt AA wasn't growing fast enough.

A man in rumpled clothes knocked at the door of the AA clubhouse in New York City. His collar was turned up, his hat was soaked. He walked with a limp. He said that he had come from St. Louis to see Bill Wilson.

The visitor was Father Ed. He told Bill that he had been reading the book *Alcoholics Anonymous* and was struck by how much the Twelve Steps looked like the Spiritual Exercises created by St. Ignatius of Loyola, the founder of the Jesuits.

A Spiritual Connection

That night, Bill Wilson and Father Ed talked for hours. Bill poured out his heart. He talked about his fears, his depression, and his struggles with pride. Father Ed listened.

When Bill confessed he felt like a total failure, Father Ed laughed. He told Bill that the winners of the world usually have too much ego to listen to God. Alcoholics were the stepchildren of the human race, and because society had kicked them to the curb, they were humble enough to be useful to God. He turned Bill's shame into his greatest asset.

This was the start of a friendship that lasted twenty years. Father Ed became Bill Wilson's spiritual advisor, or sponsor. Even though Father Ed was a Catholic priest and Bill was not a Catholic, they shared a language of the soul.

His Work with AA in St. Louis

Father Ed didn't just help Bill Wilson; he helped bring AA to the Midwest. He was one of the biggest supporters of the first AA group in St. Louis, and would often show up at meetings, sitting in the back, listening, and offering encouragement.

Father Ed never tried to turn AA into a religious organization. He understood that the power of AA was its spiritual, not religious nature. He famously said that the Twelve Steps were a way for people to find a Higher Power in a way that worked for them.

The Cana Club and Other Work

Father Ed saw that the principles of AA could also help people who weren't alcoholics. He started the Catholic Action on Narcotics and Alcohol Conference (CANA), which helped families and spouses deal with the ripple effects of addiction. He helped start groups for people with marriage problems, mental health issues, and obsessive-compulsive disorder using the Twelve Steps as a guide.

Father Ed lived the idea of attraction rather than promotion. He was joyful, even when he was in pain, had a great sense of humor, and didn't take himself too seriously.

Father Ed passed away in 1960. When he died, Bill Wilson was heartbroken. Bill wrote that Father Ed was the greatest and most gentle soul he had ever known. He credited the priest with saving his sanity and helping him keep AA on the right spiritual path during its most difficult years.

Part 5: The Storytellers & Stakeholders

Ruth Hock

The Woman Who Typed the Big Book

Ruth Hock is very difficult to categorize in the history of AA. For decades she was "merely" the secretary who typed the Big Book. In Bill and Bob's day it was common to treat secretaries as unimportant contributors to a project. That attitude would be considered unforgivably sexist today.

Working in a small office with Bill W. and Henry Parkhurst, two temperamental and opinionated personalities, Ruth Hock managed the office, produced typed drafts, edited, and physically manufactured the manuscript that would eventually become the Big Book. Bill and Hank could think, scheme, and argue, but without Ruth it would all have been empty air.

Early Life and the Job at Honor Dealers

Ruth was born in 1911 in a small town in Ohio. She had dreams and knew that a professional skill could be her ticket out of small-town Ohio. She attended a secretarial school where she mastered the high-tech tools of the 1920s: the manual typewriter and Gregg shorthand (a way of taking dictation by hand).

In the early 1930s, she moved to New York City to look for work. She landed a job at a company called Honor Dealers, the business venture started by Hank

Parkhurst. Honor Dealers was not successful, but even after it failed, she stayed on to help Bill and Hank with their side project—writing a book about how they had stopped drinking.

Ruth was witness to the office of Honor Dealers becoming the place where the Big Book was born. The pay was not steady, but it was an adventure well worth it.

Transcribing a Miracle: The Big Book

The writing of the Big Book was an arduous process, and Ruth was in it from the start. Bill would hand write a few pages at home and then take them to the office. He would then dictate from his handwritten notes. Ruth would type the pages so the boys (the early New York members) could take chapters home to tear them apart with critiques. At one point, Ruth typed the entire manuscript onto stencils for a limited printing. This resulted in about 80 copies that were sent to doctors, clergymen, and members for feedback.

Ruth witnessed the heated debates over the use of the word God versus Higher Power. She kept track of the countless revisions, organized the records, and kept the peace, even when there was no money to pay her.

Long Hours and the Birth of Alcoholics Anonymous

The period between 1938 and 1939 was a time of immense pressure. Ruth was working long hours for a project that had no funding. There were weeks when she wasn't paid at all. Her loyalty and stamina were both tested by the sheer volume of work.

Ruth was also the primary correspondent for the movement. As word spread, letters from desperate alcoholics poured in. Ruth answered each one, often being the first point of contact for people seeking help.

When the book was finally published in April 1939, it was Ruth Hock who suggested the title. The group had toyed with names like *The Way Out* and *The Empty Glass*. Ruth noted that there were already several books titled *The Way Out*, and her common sense steered the group toward naming the book after the movement itself: *Alcoholics Anonymous*.

The Manuscript and the Original Circle

Ruth remained the secretary of the Newark office and later the Vesey Street office in New York. She became a confidante to Lois Wilson, Bill's wife, and a stable maternal figure for the men of the Original Circle.

In 1940, an article in Liberty Magazine gave AA national attention. Ruth's workload became astronomical. Ruth managed thousands of inquiries, helping to coordinate the formation of new groups across the country.

In 1939, after the Alcoholics Anonymous book was published, the original limited-print manuscript—the one covered in hand-written edits, crossed-out paragraphs, and notes from Bill W.—was technically office trash.

Ruth knew the value of that office trash. She had spent nearly two years typing and re-typing those pages. When the office for Works Publishing (the precursor to AA World Services) was moving, the manuscript was going to be thrown away. Ruth, rescued it. When she left her job as AA's national secretary, Bill W. gave her the manuscript as a parting gift. For over 30 years, that historic document sat in a drawer in Ruth's home. In the late 1970s, Ruth gave it to a friend who put it up for auction. It has been in private hands since then, but copies are available for study.

Leaving the Office

In 1942, Ruth Hock left her position at the AA headquarters to get married and move to California. Her departure was a bittersweet moment for the fellowship. Bill Wilson wrote a glowing tribute to her, acknowledging that without her steadiness and dedication, the book—and perhaps the movement—might have collapsed under the weight of its own financial and emotional instability.

Even after leaving her official capacity, Ruth remained a friend of the fellowship. She often marveled at the growth of AA, noting that when she started, she knew every single member by name.

Ruth Hock (later Ruth Hock Crecelius) died on May 15, 1986. She was 74 years old.

John D. Rockefeller Jr.

The Man Who Said "No" to AA

John D. Rockefeller was one of the richest and most famous men in the world. He was not an alcoholic, but his wisdom and support played a huge part in making sure AA survived its first few years. He is most well-known for his refusal to give the new organization significant amounts of money so that it did not become distracted from its spiritual mission.

How the Connection Started

In the late 1930s, the first group of sober drunks in New York and Akron had a problem. They had found a way to stay sober, but they were penniless. Most of them had lost their jobs and their homes because of their drinking. They wanted to spread their message to other suffering alcoholics, but they didn't have the money to do it.

Bill W. had big ideas. He wanted to build hospitals for alcoholics and hire missionaries to travel and teach the program. These plans required money. One of Bill's friends, a man named Dick Richardson, worked for the Rockefeller family. Dick saw the great work the drunks were doing and arranged a meeting between the early AA members and some of Mr. Rockefeller's closest advisors.

The Famous Dinner

In 1937, a small group of early AA members went to a dinner hosted by Mr. Rockefeller's associates. They told their stories of how they had been hopeless drunks and were now sober and happy.

Mr. Rockefeller's business advisors were impressed. They sent a report to Mr. Rockefeller telling him that this new group was doing something incredible. They suggested he give them a large amount of money—perhaps $50,000 or more—to help them build their hospitals and hire their workers.

A Surprising Decision

John D. Rockefeller Jr. read the report and was also impressed. He believed in what the alcoholics were doing. However, he made a decision that shocked Bill W. at the time, but saved AA in the long run.

Mr. Rockefeller said that he would give them some help, but he would not give them a lot of money. He famously said, "I am afraid that money will spoil this thing."

He realized that if AA had too much money, it might become just another business or a professional organization. He saw that the genuine power of AA was one alcoholic talking to another alcoholic for free. He wanted the fellowship to be self-supporting and the members to keep it going themselves.

Instead of a fortune, he gave them a small gift of $5,000. He also put $3,000 of his own money into a fund to help Bill W. and Dr. Bob with their basic living expenses so they could keep working on the Big Book. This amount was just enough to keep the lights on, but not enough to change the way the program worked.

The Big Book and the Dinner of 1940

By 1940, the Big Book had been published, but it wasn't selling well. The fellowship was still struggling. Mr. Rockefeller helped again, but in a very specific way. He hosted a dinner at the Union Club in New York City, and invited many of his wealthy friends to hear about Alcoholics Anonymous.

Mr. Rockefeller could not attend because he was sick, but his son, Nelson Rockefeller, took his place. The guests heard from Bill W. and Dr. Bob. They heard the stories of recovery. At the end of the night, many of the guests expected to be asked for big donations.

But that didn't happen. Instead, Mr. Rockefeller's representative told the crowd that AA was a work of love. He told them that AA didn't need a lot of money, only their interest and their respect. This dinner gave AA the stamp of approval from the most respected people in the country.

After this dinner, news of AA spread everywhere. People started trusting the program because a man like

John D. Rockefeller Jr. supported it. The Big Book began to sell, and the fellowship grew rapidly.

Why His Role Matters

Had Mr. Rockefeller given the drunks the millions of dollars they asked for, the program might have failed. There might have been fights over money, or people might have stopped helping each other for free.

By giving only a little, he forced the early members to rely on each other and on their Higher Power. He helped create the tradition of being self-supporting through our own contributions.

An Honest and Humble Friend

John D. Rockefeller Jr. stayed in the background and let the alcoholics lead the way. He showed us that sometimes the best way to help someone is not to do everything for them, but to give them just enough help so they can learn to stand on their own feet.

In the history of AA, he is remembered as a friend of the fellowship. He didn't suffer from the disease, but he understood the spiritual heart of the program. He helped protect that heart by making sure AA stayed focused on one alcoholic helping another.

Frank Amos

John D. Rockefeller's Secret Agent

Early in the history of AA, Bill W. reached out to the famous businessman John D. Rockefeller Jr., hoping for a large donation. Mr. Rockefeller was interested, but he was also a cautious man. He didn't want to throw money at a project without knowing if it really worked.

For help, Mr. Rockefeller turned to one of the New York businessmen in his inner circle, an advertising executive named Frank Amos.

A Secret Mission to Akron

Frank was a partner in a successful advertising agency. He was not a member of the Oxford Group, and he did not have a drinking problem. What he had was a clear head for business and the trust of John D. Rockefeller.

In early 1938, AA didn't even have a name. There were just two small groups of men trying to stay sober by following spiritual principles. One group was in Akron, Ohio, led by Dr. Bob. The other was in New York, led by Bill W.

Mr. Rockefeller asked Frank Amos to go to Akron to investigate. He wanted Frank to see if these men were actually staying sober and if their program was something that could truly help others.

What Frank Found

Frank Amos arrived in Akron and spent several days there. He went to the homes of the men. He talked to their wives, and he sat in on their meetings. He talked to the doctors at the local hospital where Dr. Bob worked.

What Frank saw amazed him. He met men who had been hopeless drunks—men who had lost their jobs, their families, and their health. Now, these same men were sober, working, and happy. They were helping each other stay away from the next drink. Frank found Dr. Bob to be a man of great integrity. He saw that the Akron Group was a community built on love and service.

In his report back to Mr. Rockefeller, a report that became known as the "Amos Report," Frank wrote a seven-point summary of the program he had seen in action in Akron. The seven points were: (1) admission that the alcoholic was medically hopeless, (2) total surrender to God, (3) removal of sin, (4) morning devotions, (5) helping others, (6) meetings, and (7) church attendance.

A Change of Plans

Bill W. and the early members were hoping for millions of dollars from Mr. Rockefeller. They envisioned hospitals and hired missionaries. Frank Amos, after talking with Mr. Rockefeller, brought back a message that crushed those dreams.

Mr. Rockefeller believed that if the movement had too much money, it might lose its spiritual power. He thought that if people were paid to help alcoholics, it would ruin the one-on-one magic of the program. Instead of a huge fortune, Mr. Rockefeller gave a small amount of money to help Bill and Dr. Bob with their basic needs. At first, Bill was disappointed, but Frank Amos helped him see the wisdom in Mr. Rockefeller's decision.

Frank became a close advisor to Bill. He helped the early members set up a foundation (which later became the General Service Board) to handle what little money they had. He emphasized to them that the program should be self-supporting and run by the members themselves.

Helping Create the Big Book

Because Frank Amos was a high-level ad man, he knew the publishing world. At one point he arranged a meeting between Bill W. and Eugene Exman, the religious editor at the publishing company, Harper Brothers.

Harper Brothers offered Bill a $1,500 advance to publish the book, but Frank advised Bill against taking the deal. Instead, he encouraged the idea that AA should own its own book. Because of Frank's advice, AA formed Works Publishing and kept the rights.

The First Trustee

When the Alcoholic Foundation was formed in 1938, Frank Amos was one of the original trustees. He served on the board for many years. He wasn't there to tell the alcoholics how to stay sober; he was there to make sure the business of AA stayed honest and organized.

Frank Amos passed away in 1964.

Jack Alexander

The Reporter Who Told the World about AA

Jack Alexander was a star reporter for a famous magazine called the *Saturday Evening Post.* In 1941, he wrote an article that changed everything for AA. Before Jack's article, AA was a small group of people struggling to be heard. After his article, the whole world knew that there was hope for the hopeless drunk.

The Skeptical Reporter

Jack Alexander was born in 1902 in St. Louis, Missouri. He was a tough-as-nails journalist. Reporters are taught to be suspicious. Jack's job as a reporter was to find the truth, even if it was hidden under lies.

In 1940, Jack's editors at the *Saturday Evening Post* heard about a strange group of former drunks who claimed they had found a way to stop drinking. The idea that late-stage alcoholics could get sober by helping each other sounded like a scam to Jack.

Jack went to New York City to meet Bill W. He walked into the small AA office expecting to find a group of people trying to take money from people who were sick and suffering. He was ready to write an article that would expose them as fakes.

Finding the Truth

Jack didn't just talk to Bill W. for an hour and leave. He spent weeks investigating. He went to meetings in New York, Philadelphia, and Akron. He sat in the basements of churches and in the living rooms of members. He listened to their stories.

Jack found men and women who had lost everything—their jobs, their families, and their health—now living happy, productive lives. He saw people who used to steal and lie now practicing rigorous honesty.

Most importantly, Jack saw that AA didn't want his money or for him to make them famous. They wanted to stay sober one day at a time by helping others do the same. Jack's suspicion turned into respect. The people he met had found a medicine that no doctor had ever been able to prescribe: the power of one alcoholic talking to another.

The Article That Changed History

On March 1, 1941, the *Saturday Evening Post* published Jack's article. It was titled "Alcoholics Anonymous: Freedoms and Fetters."

The article was written so regular people could understand it. Jack described the Twelve Steps and the Big Book. He explained AA was not a religious cult, but a group of people using spiritual principles to get well. He wrote about the defects of character and the need for a higher power.

Saturday Evening Post was read by millions of people across the United States. The reaction to Jack's article was a tidal wave of interest in AA. Before the article, the AA office in New York was getting a few letters a week. After the article, they received thousands.

Mothers wrote in asking how to help their sons. Men wrote in from hotel rooms, begging for the address of the nearest meeting. Because of Jack's honest reporting, the membership of AA jumped from about 2,000 people to over 8,000 in just a few months. It was the big break the fellowship needed to survive.

A Lifelong Friend

Jack Alexander did not stop being a friend to AA after that one article. He became a non-alcoholic friend of the fellowship. He served on the Alcoholic Foundation, which later became the General Service Board.

In 1950, Jack wrote another article for the *Post.* He checked back in to see how the group was doing. He was happy to report that the experiment had worked. AA was now a worldwide movement. He saw that the principles he had written about a decade earlier were still holding strong.

Jack Alexander died in 1975. He never needed the Twelve Steps for himself, but having seen it work for so many others, he remained a supporter of AA until the end.

Bernard Smith

A Big Brother to Alcoholics Anonymous

In the early days of Alcoholics Anonymous, the movement was a small boat in a stormy ocean. Bill W. and Dr. Bob, the co-founders, knew how to help people get sober, but they were unsure how to build an organization that would last.

One of the most important people to step up for AA was Bernard Smith. Most people in AA called him Bern. He was a lawyer from New York City who never had a drinking problem, yet he dedicated much of his life to making sure AA stayed strong and safe.

A Man of Law and Logic

Bernard Smith was born in 1901. In the 1930s he was a highly successful corporate lawyer in Manhattan. He specialized in complex legal structures and negotiations.

By 1944, AA was facing a crisis of growing pains. The movement was spreading across the country, and the Alcoholic Foundation, the group that looked after the money and the Big Book, was disorganized.

Bill W. wanted a heavyweight legal mind who could handle the complex task of organizing a bunch of fiercely independent alcoholics into a structure that would last. Bill came into contact with Bernard Smith through the network of professionals that surrounded the early trustees, likely someone who had been following the AA story since the Rockefeller dinner.

Bern Smith saw in AA a spiritual movement that had the potential to change the world. He used his skills as a lawyer to help AA create a legal framework that would hold up.

The Architect of the Structure

Much of the way AA is structured today is because of the work of Bernard Smith. Originally, Bill W. was the leader. But Bill knew that for AA to survive, the power had to belong to the groups and the members, not just one or two leaders.

Bern Smith helped design the General Service Conference. This is the meeting where delegates from all over the United States and Canada come together to make decisions for AA as a whole. Bern's system viewed the conscience of the whole fellowship as more important than any single person's opinion.

He famously said that AA was an upside-down organization. In most companies, the boss is at the top. In AA, thanks to the structure Bern helped build, the individual members and groups are at the top, and the leaders are there to serve them.

The Non-Alcoholic Voice

Bern Smith had the gift of being able to talk to the public and the government in a way that made them respect AA. He served as the chairman of the General Service Board for many years. Because he wasn't an alcoholic, he could speak in public about AA without breaking the tradition of anonymity. He was the public face of the fellowship when the fellowship needed to remain hidden.

Defending the Traditions

Bernard Smith understood that if AA became too wealthy, too political, or too focused on individual personalities, it would die. He used his legal mind to help clarify why AA should never accept outside money or get involved in public controversies.

He helped the fellowship understand that its primary purpose was to stay sober and help other alcoholics. By keeping the organization simple and focused, he helped protect it from the problems that had destroyed other groups.

Bernard Smith passed away in 1970. Today, when an AA group makes a decision, or when the General Service Conference meets in New York, they are using the tools that Bernard Smith helped build. He taught the fellowship that while an alcoholic can best understand another alcoholic, it takes a community of friends—

both inside and outside the room—to make sure the hand of AA is always there.

Part 6: Voices of the Fellowship (The Circuit Speakers)

The Circuit Speakers of the 1950s

A Different Way of Carrying the Message

As Alcoholics Anonymous grew during its first twenty years, the way members shared their stories changed. Originally, AA was small. People learned the program from the founders or from the first members in New York and Akron. By the 1950s, the fellowship had thousands of members across the world. This growth led to the rise of circuit speakers.

What Were Circuit Speakers?

Circuit speakers were AA members who became well known for their ability to tell their stories in a powerful and entertaining way. Instead of just speaking at their own home groups, they were invited to travel from city to city. They spoke at large AA conventions, banquets, and regional meetings.

These speakers were very charismatic. They didn't just talk about the steps; they were performers in a sense, using humor, drama, and powerful emotions to keep the audience's attention. Because they traveled a circuit of events, they became known as circuit speakers.

How They Arose

Several things happened in the 1950s that made circuit speakers possible. First, large AA gatherings, often labeled conventions, became popular. These events needed headliner speakers who could speak to hundreds or even thousands of people at once. Second, after World War II, it became easier and cheaper to travel by plane and car. Speakers could visit many states in a short amount of time. And third, the 1950s saw the beginning of reel-to-reel tape recorders. People began to record the speakers. These tapes were then passed around from person to person. Even if you lived in a small town, you could listen to a famous speaker from Los Angeles or New York.

The Impact on AA

The circuit speakers provided great benefit, but also presented challenges.

The Positive Impact: Because they traveled so much, circuit speakers carried the same message to many places. This helped members feel like they were part of something much bigger than their local meeting. The powerful stories told by the circuit speakers gave hope to new members and reminded older members why they stayed sober. They were also excellent at explaining the Big Book in ways that were easy to understand and remember.

The Challenges: The rise of AA celebrities was an unfamiliar experience for the fellowship. AA is based on the idea of principles before personalities. Some members worried people were following the speakers rather than the program itself. There was a concern that the speaker meeting was becoming more important than the step study meeting.

A Lasting Legacy

The circuit speaker era changed AA culture. It created a tradition of high-energy storytelling that is still a big part of AA conventions today. While the speakers of the 1950s are mostly gone, their influence remains. The recordings of their talks—now on the internet instead of tapes—continue to teach new generations of members about the history and heart of the program.

Joe and Charlie

Bringing the Big Book to Life

Two men named Joe McQuany and Charlie Parmley—commonly known as Joe and Charlie—changed the way thousands of people understand the Big Book. They did not change the program, but focused on the Twelve Steps in a way that made sense to people newly struggling to stay sober.

Who Were Joe and Charlie?

Joe was a black man from Little Rock, Arkansas, who got sober in 1962. Charlie was a white man from the same area who got sober in 1963. In those days in the United States, especially in the South, it was not common for people of different races to work closely together. They met in 1973 and discovered that they both had a deep love for the book *Alcoholics Anonymous.*

They noticed that many people in AA meetings talked about their problems and their lives, but they didn't always talk about the instructions found in the Big Book. Joe and Charlie wanted people to focus on the instructions in the book.

The Start of the "Big Book Comes Alive"

Joe and Charlie began meeting at a local hotel in 1973 to study the book together. They didn't plan on becoming circuit speakers; they just wanted to understand the program better. Soon, others asked to join. These study sessions grew into what would eventually be called the "Big Book Comes Alive" seminars.

The format was simple. They would sit at a table with their Big Books open. They would read a paragraph and then explain what it meant in plain, everyday language. They used humor, personal stories, and common sense to break down the Twelve Steps for the newcomer. Charlie focused on the logic and the why of the book, while Joe combined spiritual insight with a powerful way of speaking.

Making the Program Simple

The Big Book was written in the late 1930s. As decades passed, the language seemed old-fashioned or difficult to follow. Joe and Charlie were translators. They took the old language and made it feel new.

One of their main goals was to show that AA is a program of action. They emphasized that it is not enough to sit in a meeting and listen. They walked people through the Steps exactly as they were written, showing that there was action to take. The Steps were not suggestions to think about but tasks to perform.

By using a chalkboard and simple diagrams, they illustrated ideas like the cycle of addiction in which physical craving and a mental obsession kept a person trapped. When people saw these ideas on the chalkboard, the light bulb went on for many.

Growth and Influence

Groups from outside of Little Rock started inviting Joe and Charlie to speak. For 30 years, they traveled all over the world talking about AA and the Steps.

In the 1980s and 1990s, people began recording their seminars on cassette tapes. These tapes were copied and passed from person to person. People who could never afford to travel to a seminar could listen to Joe and Charlie in their living rooms or cars. Today, in the age of digital downloads and streaming, Joe and Charlie tapes are still some of the most popular resources for people in AA.

Their Impact on AA Culture

Before Joe and Charlie, many AA meetings were discussion meetings where people shared whatever was on their mind. While this was helpful for support, some felt it lacked a focus on the actual recovery process described in the Big Book. Joe and Charlie helped start a trend of Big Book Studies. Today, thousands of AA groups have dedicated meetings where they study the text line-by-line, much like Joe and Charlie did.

An Honest Look at Their Legacy

Joe and Charlie were not official spokesmen for Alcoholics Anonymous. AA, as an organization, does not have teachers or leaders in a formal sense. Because of this, some people at the time were critical of them. Some felt that their seminars were too much like schooling and that they were making themselves too prominent.

However, Joe and Charlie were always careful to stay within the Traditions of AA. They never charged a fee, though they accepted travel expenses and sometimes sold study materials to cover costs. They always encouraged people to get involved in their local groups and to work with a sponsor.

The End of an Era

Charlie Parmley passed away in 2001, and Joe McQuany passed away in 2007. Their deaths were a great loss to the recovery community, but their work did not stop. The "Big Book Comes Alive" seminars continue through other people who have studied their methods. The tapes and transcripts of their talks continue to be used in jails, hospitals, and homes around the world.

Today, if you go to an AA meeting and see someone with a highlighted, well-worn Big Book, Joe and Charlie played a part in that. They taught a generation of people how to read, understand, and—most importantly—live the program of Alcoholics Anonymous.

Chuck Chamberlain

A New Pair of Glasses

Chuck Chamberlain was one of the most famous speakers in the history of the movement. His approach to the Twelve Steps was often described as spiritual common sense. He is best remembered for his book, *A New Pair of Glasses*, which was based on a series of talks he gave in the 1970s.

Early Life and the Problem with Drinking

Chuck was born in 1902. Like many people who eventually find their way to AA, his early life was full of promise. He was a bright and successful man who worked as a salesman in the wholesale furniture industry. As his drinking progressed, his life fell apart.

Chuck felt deeply ashamed of his alcoholism. He tried many times to stop on his own, using willpower and logic, but it never worked for long.

Finding Sobriety

Chuck entered the rooms of Alcoholics Anonymous in January 1946 in Southern California. AA was barely ten years old. The Big Book had been out for about seven years, and the program was growing rapidly on the West Coast.

When Chuck first arrived, he was a logical guy who

struggled with spiritual concepts. He soon realized that his intellectual approach to life was part of his problem. To get sober, he had to stop trying to figure everything out and instead follow a simple set of actions.

Chuck's sobriety was not just about putting the plug in the jug. He became a student of the spiritual life. He believed that the Twelve Steps were not just a way to stop drinking, but a way to change one's entire outlook on the world. This is where a new pair of glasses came from. The problem wasn't what we saw, but the lenses we were looking through.

The Impact of His Message

As Chuck gained sobriety, he became a popular speaker at AA conventions. He had a unique voice—honest, direct, and often hilarious, with an amazing ability to simplify the spiritual side of the program. He taught that "God is," and that our job is simply to get out of the way. He emphasized we do not earn sobriety or God's love; it is already there, waiting for us to accept it.

In 1975, Chuck gave a famous set of talks at a retreat in California. These talks were recorded and later transcribed into the book A *New Pair of Glasses*. Even though the book is not official AA literature (meaning it wasn't published by AA World Services), it is widely read by members of the fellowship and has remained a bestseller in the recovery community for decades.

Key Teachings

Chuck's impact can be summarized through a few of his core ideas:

1. **The Ego is the Enemy:** Chuck taught that the main problem for the alcoholic is the self. Our egos try to run the show, which leads to fear, resentment, and eventually, a drink. Sobriety, to Chuck, was the process of deflating the ego.
2. **Living in the Now:** He was an early proponent of the idea that we only have the present moment. He often told people to stop worrying about the past or the future. If we can stay sober and helpful in the now, the rest takes care of itself.
3. **The Concept of The Presence:** Instead of using complicated religious language, Chuck often talked about The Presence. He suggested that a Power greater than ourselves is always present, like the air we breathe. We don't have to go find it; we just have to become aware of it.
4. **Laughter and Joy:** Chuck thought that sobriety should be happy. He famously said, "I don't think God has a long face." He encouraged people to laugh at their own mistakes and to enjoy the broad highway of recovery.

His Legacy in AA History

Chuck Chamberlain stayed sober from 1946 until his death in 1984. For nearly 40 years, he was a pillar of the AA community in Southern California and a mentor to countless people.

Chuck stands out as a bridge between the early, pioneering days of the 1930s and the modern, global fellowship we see today. Chuck Chamberlain's story is a reminder that AA is a design for living. He didn't just want to stay sober; he wanted to be awake. By changing his perspective—getting that new pair of glasses—he gave a generation of alcoholics a way to look at the world with hope instead of fear.

Clancy Imislund

A Voice of Structure and Service

Clancy Imislund, often known simply as Clancy I., had a profound impact on the way AA is practiced, particularly in Southern California. His life is a story of a complete turnaround—from a man living on the streets to a man who led one of the largest homeless missions in the United States.

The Early Years and the Descent

Clancy was born in 1927. His relationship with alcohol began early and progressed quickly. By his late twenties, alcoholism had taken everything from him. He lost his career in advertising, his home and his connection to his family. Physically ill from drinking, he was living on the streets in the skid row district of Los Angeles.

Finding a New Path

In 1958, Clancy walked through the doors of Alcoholics Anonymous. AA was still young but had a strong presence in Southern California. Clancy didn't want to stop drinking at first—he just couldn't keep living the way he was.

Clancy found a sponsor and took the Twelve Steps at the Midnight Mission in Los Angeles. This mission served the poorest and most desperate people in the city. When Clancy got sober, he didn't leave the Mission. Instead, he dedicated his life to it. He eventually became its managing director, a position he held for decades. As director, he transformed the mission from a simple soup kitchen into a comprehensive recovery and transition center..

The Pacific Group

Clancy is perhaps famous—and controversial—for his role in the Pacific Group. This is an AA group in West Los Angeles that grew to be one of the largest in the world. Under Clancy's leadership, the Pacific Group developed a very ordered way of practicing the AA program.

The Pacific Group is known for its Blue Card system and a high level of structure. The group had firm suggestions (some say strict rules) about how members should dress for meetings--usually in suits or formal wear--and how they should conduct themselves. The dress code was part of acting one's way into right thinking. Clancy taught that if alcoholics who had lived chaotic and messy lives began to take pride in their appearance and follow strict rules, their inner lives would eventually do the same.

Some members of AA felt Clancy's approach was too rigid or didn't fit the informal nature of the fellowship. Others credited Clancy and the Pacific Group strictness with saving their lives. He emphasized that alcoholism was a deadly disease, and recovery needed to be taken with absolute seriousness.

His Impact on the Fellowship

Clancy became a sought-after speaker at AA conventions across the globe. He was known for his wit, his sharp humor, and his ability to tell a story that made people laugh while delivering a hard truth. He had a way of describing the alcoholic ego that resonated with newcomers and old-timers alike.

Through his work at the Midnight Mission, he showed that the principles of AA could be used to run a major non-profit organization. Clancy was a firm believer in the power of one alcoholic working with another. He insisted on a very active form of sponsorship where the sponsor was deeply involved in the newcomer's life. He taught that recovery was about more than just not drinking; it was about becoming a productive, responsible member of society. For him, that started with making your bed and showing up on time.

A Legacy of Tough Love

Clancy Imislund passed away in 2020 with over 61 years of continuous sobriety. To some, he was a polarizing figure because he was never afraid to speak his mind or tell an alcoholic that they were full of it.

However, his tough love approach was always rooted in a deep desire to see people get well. He knew what it was like to sleep on a sidewalk, and he knew what it was like to have his life restored. In the history of AA, Clancy remains a symbol of the Old School approach. He treated the Big Book as a textbook to be followed, not a collection of suggestions to be accepted or ignored. He reminded the fellowship that while AA is a program of attraction, doing that program requires discipline and hard work.

Sandy Beach

A Voice of Joy and Simplicity

As AA matured, new voices emerged to help explain the AA program to newer generations. One of the most beloved and influential of these voices was a man named Willard M. Beacham. He is better known in AA history as Sandy Beach.

Through thousands of recorded talks, Sandy helped bridge the gap between the old-fashioned language of the 1930s and the modern world.

Early Life and the Struggle

Sandy Beach was born in 1931. He served in the United States Marine Corps and later found success as a lobbyist in Washington, D.C. As a lobbyist, drinking was a social lubricant and political tool. But for Sandy it became a daily necessity.

Sandy entered Alcoholics Anonymous on December 7, 1964. His sobriety date, Pearl Harbor Day, became an important part of his story. His life had been bombed by alcohol, but through AA he turned that day of infamy into a day of freedom.

In early recovery, Sandy struggled with the spiritual nature of the program. He was a man of intellect, and the idea of surrendering to a Higher Power didn't come easily. He eventually had a breakthrough when he realized that his own best thinking had led him to a life of misery. Finally, he could set aside his ego and try the Twelve Steps as they were written.

The Plain and Simple Message

As Sandy grew in his sobriety, he began to speak at AA conventions and meetings. He had a knack for making complex spiritual concepts sound like common sense.

Sandy refused to let recovery be grim. If we can't laugh at our own mistakes, he pointed out, we aren't really growing. His talks were famous for being hilarious. He would tell stories of his alcoholic logic that made listeners laugh until they cried. With humor, he broke down the defenses of people who were scared or ashamed, and showed them that they weren't bad people. They were people with a sickness who were trying to get better.

Sandy often talked about the ego. He explained that for an alcoholic, the ego is a filter that distorts reality. The main goal of the Twelve Steps is to reduce the ego so that a person can connect with others and with a Higher Power. He often used the analogy that the ego wants to be the director of the movie, but the program teaches us to be one of the actors.

Sandy kept it simple. He focused on the idea that Step One is about realizing we can't control our drinking, and the rest of the steps are about learning how to live without having to control everything else.

The Impact of His Recorded Talks

During the 1970s, 1980s, and 1990s, the circuit speaking culture of AA grew. People began recording talks on cassette tapes and sharing them.

Sandy's talks, such as his famous "Best of Sandy B." and his "Twelve Step Workshop," became some of the most widely circulated recordings in recovery history. Before the internet, these tapes were passed from person to person after meetings. For many in remote areas, Sandy's voice on a cassette tape was their first real connection to AA.

Even today, in the digital age, his talks are downloaded from the internet millions of times a year. He has a way of speaking directly to the new person, making them feel like they belong.

Impact on AA Philosophy

Sandy helped shift the vibe of AA in the later part of the 20th century by moving away from a fire and brimstone style toward a message of joy and freedom. He said that sobriety is more than just not drinking. If you stop drinking but stay angry, selfish, and miserable, you haven't really found recovery—you've just changed seats on the Titanic.

Later Life and Legacy

Sandy Beach stayed sober for over 50 years. He remained active in the program until his death in 2014. He didn't just talk about the steps; he lived them. Even as an elderly man with decades of sobriety, he would still attend his home group and talk to newcomers.

Part 8: Keepers of the Legacy (Literature, History, and Family)

The Heartbeat of AA: The Literature

Alcoholics Anonymous is a program of action. But if you look at how that action is shared, it is also a program of words. The people who started AA knew that they couldn't be everywhere at once, so they needed a way to share their experience, strength, and hope with people they might never meet in person.

Today, AA publishes books, pamphlets, and magazines. There is the Big Book, the *Twelve Steps and Twelve Traditions* (often called the 12x12), and the "AA Grapevine." This literature is the voice of the fellowship.

The Big Book

In 1938, AA was tiny. There were only about 100 sober members, mostly in Akron and New York. Bill W. realized that if the message was going to spread and not be diluted as it went from person to person, it had to be written down.

Bill was often broke and stressed. He wrote chapters and sent them to the members in Akron and New York. They argued over almost every word. Some members wanted the book to be very religious, using lots of thees and thous. Others, who were atheists or agnostics, wanted it to be scientific.

The result of this conflict was a masterpiece of balance. The book became inclusive. Instead of demanding that everyone believe in a specific God, they used the phrase "God *as we understood Him*." This opened the door for those who had been turned off by organized religion but still needed a spiritual solution to their drinking problem.

When the book was published in 1939, its official title was *Alcoholics Anonymous*. Because the paper was so thick (to make the book look like a good value for the money), people started calling it the Big Book. It contained the Twelve Steps for the first time in their final form. It also included personal stories so that readers could see themselves in the pages.

The Twelve Steps and Twelve Traditions (The 12x12)

By the early 1950s, AA had grown from 100 people to thousands. With growth came new problems. How should groups be run? How should they handle money? Who is in charge?

Bill W. wrote the *Twelve Steps and Twelve Traditions* in 1952 to answer these questions. While the Big Book is about how to get sober, the 12x12 is more about how to stay sober and live together.

The first half of the 12x12 dives deeper into the Steps, and is a bit more philosophical than the Big Book. It talks about things like humility, resentment, and emotional sobriety. The second half focuses on the Twelve Traditions. These are the guardrails that keep AA groups from falling apart. They teach us about anonymity, self-support, and our primary purpose: to stay sober and help other alcoholics.

The AA Grapevine: A Meeting in Print

In June 1944, a small group of members in New York started a newsletter. They called it the AA *Grapevine*. They wanted a way to share news and stories between meetings. Bill W. loved the idea and often published articles in it about the future of the fellowship.

The Grapevine is a meeting in print. Every month, it features stories written by regular members, showing that the program is alive and changing. It deals with modern problems: how to stay sober during a divorce, how to handle grief, or how to practice the steps at work.

In the 1980s, the fellowship decided that the Grapevine was so important that it should be called the "International Journal of Alcoholics Anonymous." It is a reminder that the message isn't just in old books; it is happening right now, in the lives of people sitting in meetings today.

Other Important Literature

As the years went by, AA realized that different people have different needs.

- **Daily Reflections:** This is a book of 365 readings, one for each day of the year. It was written by members for members. It is a simple way to start the day by focusing on recovery.
- **As Bill Sees It:** This is a collection of Bill W.'s writings from many different sources. It's great for when you only have five minutes and need a spiritual lift.
- **Living Sober:** This is a very practical book. It doesn't talk much about God or Spirituality. Instead, it gives tips on how not to drink today. It covers things like what to do at a party, how to handle the jitters, and the importance of eating something sweet when you have a craving.
- **Pamphlets:** AA has dozens of pamphlets. Some are for specific groups, like "AA for the Black and African-American Alcoholic," "AA for the Older Member," or "LGBTQ Alcoholics in AA." The pamphlets ensure no one feels left out.

Where the Literature Comes From Today

A common question is: "Who writes this stuff now that the founders are gone?"

AA literature is service material that belongs to the fellowship as a whole.

1. **The General Service Conference:** Every year, representatives from all over the U.S. and Canada

meet in New York. These are regular members who have been elected by their local groups. They are the voice and conscience of AA.

2. **The Literature Committee:** If a group thinks we need a new book or a change to a pamphlet, they send a suggestion to the Conference. The Literature Committee looks at it.
3. **The Process:** Nothing gets changed or published without a vote. This is why it takes a long time for new AA books to come out. For example, the project to create a "Plain Language Big Book" took years of discussion and voting to make sure the original message wasn't lost.
4. **AA World Services (AAWS):** This is the business side that handles the actual printing and distribution. But it don't own the words—AA does.

The "Plain Language" Evolution

Recently, the fellowship has worked on a "Plain Language" version of the Big Book. The original Big Book was written in the language of the 1930s. Some people today find it difficult to understand.

The goal of the plain language version is not to change the meaning of the steps, but to make sure the door to the steps is wide open. If a person is shaking, scared, and can't focus, they need the message to be as clear as possible. AA has always adapted to reach the still-suffering alcoholic, and this is just the latest way of doing that.

Why Literature Matters

You might ask, "Can't I just go to meetings? Why do I need to read?"

Meetings are where we find the heart of AA, but the literature is where we find the map. In a meeting, someone might give you terrible advice or share something that isn't really AA. If you have the books, you can always consult the source.

The literature also helps when a person is alone. Many alcoholics have stayed sober in places where there were no meetings—on ships at sea, in prison cells, or in remote towns—simply because they had a Big Book. The books and the literature are a portable sponsor. They are there at 3:00 AM when the world feels dark and the phone feels heavy.

Richmond Walker

The Man Behind the Little Black Book

Richmond Walker was born in 1892 into a well-to-do family in New England, where he had every advantage. He was well-educated, graduating from Williams College, and possessed a natural talent for writing and business. To those who knew him in his youth, Rich, as he was often called, seemed destined for a life of success and respectability.

He married, had children, and built a career in the advertising business. However, beneath the surface of this successful life, a shadow was growing. Richmond Walker could not handle alcohol the way other people did.

The Descent

At first, drinking was just a part of his social and professional life. But over time, the social aspect disappeared, leaving only the need to drink. The very traits that made him a success in business—his focus and his drive—turned against him when it came to alcohol.

By the late 1930s, Richmond's life was falling apart. His health was failing, his relationships were strained, and his career was in jeopardy. He was a man who valued order and logic, yet his life was in chaos. He reached a point of pitiful and incomprehensible demoralization.

Finding a New Way

In 1939, the same year the Big Book was published, Richmond Walker became one of the very first members of the Alcoholics Anonymous group in Boston. AA was still small. There were no old-timers to guide him. The members were all learning together, relying on the principles laid out by Bill W. and Dr. Bob.

Richmond took to the program with a deep, quiet passion. He realized that for him, the key to staying sober was not just staying away from a drink, but changing the way he thought and lived. He practiced the Twelve Steps with the same precision he once applied to his business life.

The Need for a Daily Guide

As the Boston group grew, Richmond noticed that while the Big Book was a master text for recovery, many people struggled with how to apply its principles to their everyday lives, hour by hour. They needed something short, simple, and portable—something they could look at in the morning to set their mindset for the day.

In the early 1940s, Richmond began putting together a small collection of thoughts. He was looking for a way to help himself and his friends in the Boston group stay focused on their recovery.

He gathered materials from the Big Book, religious devotionals, and quiet time meditations used by the Oxford Group, and organized them into a thought for the day, a meditation, and a prayer.

Twenty-Four Hours a Day

Richmond's collection became a small book titled *Twenty-Four Hours a Day*. Because of its size and the color of its cover, it became known as The Little Black Book.

The book focused on a simple but powerful idea: anyone can stay sober for just one day. If a person could focus on the next twenty-four hours without worrying about the past or fearing the future, they had a chance.

At first, the book was printed privately for the Boston group. But as members traveled to other cities, they took their Little Black Books with them. Word spread quickly. Other AA groups began asking for copies. Richmond eventually gave the rights to the book to the Hazelden Foundation so that it could be distributed to anyone who needed it.

A Legacy of Service

Even though he wrote one of the most important books in recovery history, Richmond Walker remained a humble member of AA, often sitting in the back of meetings and listening to newcomers. While the Big

Book provided the map for recovery, Richmond's book provided the daily bread.

His Final Years

Richmond Walker stayed sober until he passed away in 1965. Every morning, in kitchens, offices, and treatment centers all over the world, people open *Twenty-Four Hours a Day* to find the strength to stay sober for one more day.

Nell Wing

The Keeper of the History

For over thirty years, Nell Wing was the personal secretary to Bill W. Later, she became the fellowship's first official archivist. Without her, much of the history of how AA began might have been lost forever.

Early Life and Finding a Job

Nell was born in 1917 and grew up in New Jersey. In 1947, she was looking for work in New York City. She heard about a job opening at a place called the Alcoholic Foundation. She didn't know much about alcoholism or the program of AA. She just needed a job and was a good typist.

When she first walked into the small office, AA was still very young. The Big Book had been out for less than ten years. The office was busy, crowded, and full of energy. Nell was hired as a secretary.

Working with Bill W.

Nell soon became the person Bill W. relied on the most. He was constantly writing letters, working on new books, and thinking about how to keep AA unified. Nell kept his life organized. She typed his drafts, managed his mail, and made sure he stayed on track.

Working for Bill wasn't easy. He could be intense and

often worked late into the night. Nell brought a calm presence to the office. She saw Bill not as a saint, but as a human being with strengths and weaknesses. She respected him deeply, but she also saw him struggle with depression and the weight of leading a growing movement.

Nell saw history happen in real time. She was there when the Twelve Traditions were being debated. She was there when the General Service Conference was formed.

Becoming the Archivist

As the years went by, Nell noticed something important. Many of the original letters, notes, and records of AA were being kept in old boxes or even thrown away. She saw that if someone didn't save these things, future generations would lose the true story of how AA started.

She gathered papers. She saved old photographs. She kept copies of the very first editions of the Big Book. Bill W. encouraged her. He didn't want the history of AA to become a set of myths or legends. He wanted people to know the truth about how things started.

In 1970, AA officially created the Archives, and Nell was chosen to lead it. She stopped being a secretary and became the first archivist of Alcoholics Anonymous. She spent the rest of her career organizing documents.

A Non-Alcoholic Friend

One of the most remarkable things about Nell Wing was her dedication to anonymity. Even though she wasn't an alcoholic, she lived by many of the program's principles, by staying humble and out of the spotlight.

Nell loved the people in AA. She often said that being around AA members made her a better person. She saw people come into the office at their lowest point—broken and hopeless—and watched them transform into happy, useful human beings. This gave her a deep sense of purpose.

Nell was also very honest. In her later years, she wrote a book about her time with Bill W. called *Grateful to Have Been There*. In it, she spoke plainly about the early days. She didn't hide the mistakes or the arguments that happened in the office. She believed that the history of AA was beautiful because it was human. She wanted people to know that the founders weren't perfect, which meant that anyone could find recovery, no matter their flaws.

Her Legacy

Nell Wing retired in 1983, but she never truly left AA. She continued to travel and speak at conventions, sharing stories about the early days. She helped other countries start their own archives. She wanted every AA group in the world to understand where they came from.

When Nell passed away in 2007 at the age of 90, the AA community felt a great loss. She had been the memory of the fellowship.

How AA is Organized Today

Most people think of an organization like a tall building. The boss sits at the top, and tells everyone else what to do. The orders go down from the top floor to the basement. But Alcoholics Anonymous is different. It is an upside-down organization. In AA, the most important people are the members in the local groups. The leaders are at the bottom, and they are there to serve the groups, not to rule them.

This way of doing things can seem strange at first. How can thousands of groups stay together without a president or a board of directors giving orders? The answer is found in the Twelve Traditions and the Twelve Concepts for World Service. These guides help the Fellowship work together in peace.

The Home Group: Where It All Begins

Everything in AA starts with the group. A group is just two or more alcoholics meeting together for sobriety. Each group is autonomous. This means the group may manage its own affairs. A group can decide when to meet, what kind of coffee to serve, and how to run its meetings.

The group is the ultimate authority in AA. The groups own AA and decide what happens to the Fellowship as a whole. They do this by talking things over and finding a group conscience. When members meet with a spirit of love and service, a higher power speaks through the collective voice.

The General Service Representative (G.S.R.)

Because a group is busy helping the next person who walks through the door, it cannot spend all its time worrying about AA in other cities or countries. To stay connected, each group elects a member called a General Service Representative, or G.S.R.

The G.S.R. is the link between the group and the rest of the world. They take the group's feelings and ideas to larger meetings, and bring back news about how AA is doing elsewhere. The G.S.R. is a trusted servant. They do not have the power to tell the group what to do, but they have the responsibility to represent the group's heart and mind.

Districts and Areas

To keep things organized, groups that are close to each other form a District. The G.S.R.s from these groups meet regularly to talk about local problems, like how to get AA books into local hospitals or jails. They elect a leader called a District Committee Member (D.C.M.).

Districts then join to form an Area. An Area usually covers a whole state or a large part of a province. Each

Area has an Assembly where all the G.S.R.s and D.C.M.s meet. This is where the big decisions are made for that region. Once every two years, the Area elects a Delegate. This person is an experienced member who represents the Area at the big yearly meeting in New York.

The General Service Conference

Once a year, all the Delegates from across the United States and Canada meet for the General Service Conference. They are joined by the people who work at the main AA office and the people who look after the Fellowship's money and legal affairs.

This Conference is the closest thing AA has to a government, but the Conference cannot make rules for the local groups. Instead, they talk about things that affect AA as a whole. They might discuss whether to change a few words in a pamphlet or how to handle AA on the internet. They look for substantial unanimity, which means they make sure almost everyone agrees before they act. This prevents a small group of people from forcing their will on everyone else.

The General Service Board and General Service Office

At the very bottom of the upside-down pyramid are the Trustees of the General Service Board and the workers at the General Service Office (G.S.O.) in New York. Both are parts of a 501(c)(3) organization called the General Service Board of Alcoholics Anonymous, Inc. The organization is a charity, so it does not pay taxes,, but unlike most charities, it does not do money-raising activities.

The Trustees of the General Service Board are the guardians of AA. There are 21 of them. Fourteen of them are alcoholics, and seven are non-alcoholic friends (like doctors or lawyers) who support AA and want to help. Their job is to look after the history, funds, and public image of the Fellowship. They make sure the Big Book stays the way it was written and that the message remains clear.

The G.S.O. is the service center. If a group in a small town needs help, they can write to the G.S.O. The workers there—many of whom are AA members—will share the experiences of other groups. They also handle the printing of books and translating AA literature into many languages.

This board oversees two other corporate entities that also hold 501(c)(3) status. The first affiliated corporation is Alcoholics Anonymous World Services, Inc. This branch publishes the Big Book and all other official literature. The second affiliated corporation is AA Grapevine, Inc. This entity publishes the international journal of the fellowship.

Why It Works: Rotation and Self-Support

Two things keep this structure healthy: rotation and being self-supporting.

Rotation means that no one stays in a service job forever. Most jobs last for two years. When the time is up, the person steps down and someone else takes over. This keeps personalities from becoming more important than principles. It makes sure that no one person becomes the boss of a group or a district.

Being self-supporting means that AA takes no outside money and limits the amount that can be accepted from members. At the time of writing this book, individual contributions are limited to $5,000. One-time bequests by will or trust are limited to $10,000. No money is accepted from the government, foundations, other charities, or people who are not members of AA. Groups pay their own way through the small contributions members put in the basket at meetings. This keeps AA free. Because the Fellowship does not owe anyone anything, it is never forced to change its message to please a donor.

The Spirit of Service

The organizational structure of AA exists for one purpose: to help the alcoholic who is still suffering. Committees, delegates, and offices are maintained so that when someone reaches out for help, the hand of AA is always there.

AA is a fellowship of equals. From the newest member in their first meeting to the Delegate at the Conference, all are simply alcoholics trying to stay sober and help others. The structure is not built on power, but on love and the desire to be of service. By staying organized in this simple, upside-down way, the Fellowship ensures that AA will be here for as long as there are people who need it.

Glossary of AA Terms

Alcoholics Anonymous has its own way of talking about recovery. This glossary explains some of the most common words and phrases you will find in this book and hear in meetings.

AA World Services (AAWS): The business side of the fellowship. They handle the printing of books and making sure the message of AA is available in many languages.

Al-Anon: A separate fellowship for the families and friends of alcoholics. It was started by Lois Wilson (Bill's wife) and Anne Binney.

Alcoholic Foundation: The original name for the group of people who looked after AA's money and records. Today, it is called the General Service Board.

Anonymity: The idea that principles come before personalities. Members do not share their last names or faces in the media (like TV or newspapers) to protect their privacy and the reputation of AA

The Big Book: The nickname for the book *Alcoholics Anonymous*. It is the main textbook of the program and contains the Twelve Steps and many personal stories of recovery.

Bleeding Deacon: A slang term for an older member of

a group who is very resistant to change. They often believe their way is the only right way and may complain loudly when the group decides to do things differently. While they can be difficult, they often act out of a deep love for the fellowship.

Business Meeting: A separate gathering where AA members discuss the earthly needs of their group. They talk about things like paying the rent, buying coffee, and electing new people for service positions. This keeps the regular recovery meetings focused on staying sober.

Chair: This is both a verb and a noun in AA To "chair" a meeting means to lead it. The "Chair" is the person sitting at the front who starts the meeting, keeps time, and calls on people to speak. Like the Secretary, this is a service position that rotates often.

Class A and Class B Trustees: The leaders on the General Service Board. Class A trustees are non-alcoholics (like doctors or lawyers). Class B trustees are members of AA (alcoholics).

Closed Meeting: A meeting that is only for people who have a desire to stop drinking.

Conference-Approved: A label given to books and pamphlets that have been voted on and officially accepted by the General Service Conference.

Cross Talk: A behavior discouraged in many AA meetings where one member interrupts or talks directly to another person while they are sharing. Most groups prefer that members speak only to the whole room to keep the meeting orderly and safe.

DCM (District Committee Member): An experienced AA member who leads a "District" (a group of several AA meetings in a local area). The DCM helps the individual groups stay connected to the rest of AA

Doctor's Opinion: The opening section of the Big Book, written by Dr. William D. Silkworth. In it, he explains the allergy theory—the idea that alcoholics have a physical reaction to alcohol that makes it impossible for them to stop once they start.

Dry Drunk: A term used to describe a person who has stopped drinking but still acts in the angry, selfish, or dishonest ways they did while using alcohol. It means the person has physical sobriety but has not yet experienced a change in their character or attitude.

The Four Horsemen: A phrase found in the Big Book that describes the four terrible feelings that haunt an alcoholic: Terror, Bewilderment, Frustration, and Despair.

Functioning Alcoholic: A person who is able to keep their job, family, and home while still drinking heavily. To the outside world, they seem to have their life together, but they are often suffering from the same mental obsession and physical allergy as any other alcoholic.

General Service Conference: A yearly meeting in New York where members from across the United States and Canada make big decisions for the future of AA

General Service Office (GSO): The main office for AA located in New York City. They help groups all over the world.

GSR (General Service Representative): A member chosen by their home group to represent that group's voice at local and area meetings. The GSR is the link between the individual meeting and AA as a whole.

High Bottom: A term for someone who seeks help for their drinking before they lose everything. They may still have a job and a family, but they realize that their drinking is becoming a problem they cannot control on their own.

Higher Power: A power greater than oneself. In AA, every person gets to choose their own conception of this power, whether they call it God, the AA group, or nature.

Hitting Bottom: The moment when an alcoholic realizes they can no longer live with their drinking and becomes willing to try anything to stop. For some, this is a major loss; for others, it is simply a deep feeling of hopelessness.

Home Group: The specific AA meeting that a member attends most often and where they feel they belong.

Low Bottom: A term for an alcoholic who has lost everything—their home, their family, their health, or their freedom—before they finally ask for help.

Maintenance Drinker: A person who drinks small amounts of alcohol throughout the day to keep from feeling sick or having withdrawals. They rarely seem very drunk, but they are never completely sober.

Open Meeting: A meeting where anyone can attend, including family members or students who want to learn about AA

Original Circle: The small group of the first AA members in Akron and New York who worked together to build the fellowship before the Big Book was published in 1939.

Oxford House: A type of self-run, self-supported recovery house started in 1975. Residents live together democratically, pay their own rent, and must leave immediately if they use drugs or alcohol. While independent from AA, many residents use the Twelve Steps to stay sober.

Oxford Group: A Christian movement that was popular in the 1930s. The early members of AA learned many of their spiritual tools (like honesty and making amends) from this group.

The Pacific Group: A large and well-known AA group in California famous for its strict adherence to traditions and its formal way of running meetings.

Periodic Drinker: A person who can go for weeks or months without a drink but then goes on a binge where they cannot stop for several days. Even though they don't drink every day, they have no control once they start.

The Preamble: A short paragraph read at the start of most meetings that explains what AA is and that it doesn't take sides in outside fights.

Secretary: A member chosen by an AA group to handle the day-to-day business of the meeting. This person usually opens the room, makes announcements, and finds speakers. Being a secretary is a service position, not a position of power.

Self-Supporting: The rule that AA only takes money from its own members and refuses outside donations or government grants. This keeps the program independent.

Service Work: Any action taken to help AA as a whole

or to help another alcoholic stay sober. This can be as simple as making coffee at a meeting or as complex as serving on a national committee. In AA, helping others is considered a vital part of staying sober.

Seventh Tradition: The guideline that states AA should be fully self-supporting, declining outside contributions. It is why meetings pass the hat to pay for rent and coffee, and why AA refuses big checks from people who aren't members.

Share: In a meeting, to share means to tell your story or talk about your experience with recovery. When a member is called on, they share their hope and strength with the rest of the group.

Slip: A slang term for a brief return to drinking after a period of sobriety. In AA, it is often said that a slip starts in the mind long before the person actually picks up a drink.

Spiritual Experience: A change in the way a person thinks and feels that allows them to recover from alcoholism. For some, like Bill W., it is a sudden flash. For most others, it is a slow educational change that happens over time by working the Twelve Steps.

Sponsorship: A one-on-one relationship where a person with more time in sobriety (a sponsor) helps a newcomer (a sponsee) work through the Twelve Steps.

Step Study: A type of AA meeting where the members focus specifically on reading and discussing the Twelve Steps, usually one step per week.

Thirteenth Step: A slang term used to describe when a long-time member tries to start a romantic or sexual relationship with a newcomer. This is generally discouraged because it can distract the newcomer from their recovery and is seen as taking advantage of someone when they are vulnerable.

The Twelve Concepts: A set of principles that guide how AA provides service and how the different parts of the organization relate to each other. They ensure that the groups always have the final authority.

The Twelve Steps: The core program of recovery. They are a series of actions that help a person change their character and stay sober.

The Twelve Traditions: The rules that keep AA groups healthy and united. They deal with things like money, leadership, and how AA talks to the public.

White Light Experience: A term used to describe a sudden, powerful, and dramatic spiritual awakening. It refers to Bill Wilson's experience in Towns Hospital where he felt a great sense of light and peace.

Works Publishing: The tiny company that Bill W. and Hank P. started to publish the first Big Book because no regular publisher wanted to take the risk.

www.ingramcontent.com/pod-product-compliance
Lightning Source LLC
LaVergne TN
LVHW041928090826
845145LV00017B/2298